First World War
and Army of Occupation
War Diary
France, Belgium and Germany

7 INDIAN (MEERUT) DIVISION
19 (Dehra Dun) Indian Infantry Brigade
1/9 Battalion Gurkha Rifles
9 August 1914 - 30 November 1915

WO95/3941/3

The Naval & Military Press Ltd
www.nmarchive.com
Published in association with The National Archives

Published by

The Naval & Military Press Ltd

Unit 10 Ridgewood Industrial Park,

Uckfield, East Sussex,

TN22 5QE England

Tel: +44 (0) 1825 749494

www.naval-military-press.com

www.nmarchive.com

This diary has been reprinted in facsimile from the original. Any imperfections are inevitably reproduced and the quality may fall short of modern type and cartographic standards.

© Crown Copyright
Images reproduced by permission of The National Archives, London, England, 2015.

Contents

Document type	Place/Title	Date From	Date To
Heading	WO95/3941/3 1/9 Battalion Gurkha Rifles		
Heading	Meerut Division Dehradun Brigade 1-9th Gurkha Rifles 1914 Aug-1915 Nov To Mesopotamia 3 Lahore Div 9 Bde		
Miscellaneous	Meerut Division Aug-Dec 1914 1/9th Gurkha Rifles		
Diagram etc	Part B7		
Heading	War Diary of 1/9th Gurkha Rifles From 9/6/14 To 27-10-14 Volume I		
War Diary	Dehradun	09/08/1914	01/09/1914
War Diary	Bombay	04/09/1914	03/10/1914
War Diary	Port Said	04/10/1914	11/10/1914
War Diary	Marseilles	12/10/1914	12/10/1914
War Diary	Camp Valentine Marseilles	13/10/1914	19/10/1914
War Diary	Orleans	20/10/1914	26/10/1914
War Diary	On Train.	27/10/1914	27/10/1914
War Diary	Merville	27/10/1914	27/10/1914
War Diary	Entrainment At Marseilles.	17/10/1914	24/10/1914
Heading	War Diary of 1/9th Gurkha Rifles From 28-10-14 To 12-1-15		
War Diary	Merville	28/10/1914	28/10/1914
War Diary	Vielle Chapelle.	29/10/1914	30/10/1914
War Diary	N.W. Of Neuve Chapelle	30/10/1914	30/10/1914
War Diary	Trenches Pont Logy	31/10/1914	14/11/1914
War Diary	Vielle Chapelle	15/11/1914	21/11/1914
War Diary	Richebourg L'Avoue, Trenches	22/11/1914	23/11/1914
War Diary	Lehamel-Lillets	24/11/1914	27/11/1914
War Diary	Billets Near Festubert	28/11/1914	02/12/1914
War Diary	Left Section Trenches Festubert	03/12/1914	15/12/1914
War Diary	Billets rue De Lepinetie	16/12/1914	20/12/1914
War Diary	Orchard Trenches S.E Of Rue De Lepinette	20/12/1914	22/12/1914
War Diary	Trenches Rue De Lepinette	22/12/1914	27/12/1914
War Diary	Billets Bailleul	28/12/1914	12/01/1915
Heading	War Diary of 1/9th Gurkhas From 13th January 1915 To 29th January 1915		
War Diary	Billets Bailleul Aux Pernes	13/01/1915	26/01/1915
War Diary	Billets Vielle Chapelle	27/01/1915	29/01/1915
Operation(al) Order(s)	Operation Order No. 12 by Brigadier General C.W. Jacob Commanding Dehra Dun Brigade	20/01/1915	20/01/1915
Miscellaneous	Head Quarters Dehradun Brigade	22/01/1915	22/01/1915
Operation(al) Order(s)	Operation Order No. 13 by Brigadier General C.W. Jacob Commanding Dehra Dun Brigade	23/01/1915	23/01/1915
Operation(al) Order(s)	Operation Order No. 14 by Brigadier General C.W. Jacob Commanding Dehra Dun Brigade	28/01/1915	28/01/1915
Miscellaneous	9th Gurkhas		
Heading	War Diary With Appendix B 1/9th Gurkha Rifles. From 30th January 1915 To 26th February 1915.		
War Diary	Billets-Rue Des Berceaux	30/01/1915	02/02/1915
War Diary	Trenches Richebourg St Vaast.	02/02/1915	04/02/1915
War Diary	Billets Vielle Chapelle	05/02/1915	13/02/1915
War Diary	Billets. Quentin.	14/02/1915	23/02/1915

Type	Description	Start	End
War Diary	Billets Richebourg St. Vaast	24/01/1915	26/02/1915
Miscellaneous	Daily Report	02/02/1915	02/02/1915
Miscellaneous	To adjutant 1/9th L.R.	02/02/1915	02/02/1915
Miscellaneous	Operation Orders. By No 3 Company Daily Report	03/11/1915	03/11/1915
Miscellaneous	Adjutant	03/02/1915	03/02/1915
Miscellaneous	To O.C. 9th Gurkhas		
Miscellaneous	Daily Reports No. 3 Company	04/02/1915	04/02/1915
Miscellaneous	Adjutant 1/9 Gurkha Rifles		
Miscellaneous	To O C 9th Gurkhas	04/02/1915	04/02/1915
Miscellaneous	The Adjutant 1/9th	04/02/1915	04/02/1915
Miscellaneous	To Adjutant	04/02/1915	04/02/1915
Miscellaneous	Garhwal Report On Right Sub-Station C2		
Miscellaneous	Report		
War Diary	Trenches Richebourg St. Vaast	01/02/1915	04/02/1915
Map	Map		
War Diary	Trenches Richebourg St Vaast	01/02/1915	04/02/1915
Map	Map		
Operation(al) Order(s)	Operation Order No. 15 by Brigadier General C.W. Jacob C.B. Commanding Dehra Dun Brigade	31/01/1915	31/01/1915
Miscellaneous	Operation Orders by Lt. Col. G.T. Widdicombe Commanding 9th Goorkhas. Appendix B.	02/02/1915	02/02/1915
Miscellaneous	D D Bde	02/02/1915	02/02/1915
Miscellaneous	D D Bde		
Operation(al) Order(s)	Operation Order No. 16 by Brigadier General C.W. Jacob Commanding Dehra Dun Brigade	03/02/1915	03/02/1915
Miscellaneous	A Form. Messages And Signals. Appendix B		
Miscellaneous	Operation Orders by Lt. Col. G.T. Widdicombe Commanding C.2 Section. Appendix B	04/02/1915	04/02/1915
Operation(al) Order(s)	Operation Order No. 17 by Brigadier General C.W. Jacob Commanding Dehra Dun Brigade	07/02/1915	07/02/1915
Operation(al) Order(s)	Operation Order No. 18 by Brigadier General C.W. Jacob Commanding Dehra Dun Brigade	20/02/1915	20/02/1915
Miscellaneous	Dehradun Brigade		
Miscellaneous			
Operation(al) Order(s)	Operation Order No. 19 by Brigadier General C.W. Jacob Commanding Dehra Dun Brigade	21/02/1915	21/02/1915
Heading	War Diary of 1/9th Gurkha Rifles From Feb 27th 1915 & 27th March 1915 Pages 38-49.		
War Diary	Billets Richebourg St Vaast	27/02/1915	02/03/1915
War Diary	Trenches Rue Du Bois B Sub Section	02/03/1915	02/03/1915
War Diary	Billets Vielle Chapelle	03/03/1915	10/03/1915
War Diary	Dusk	10/03/1915	13/03/1915
War Diary	Les Lobes	14/03/1915	24/03/1915
War Diary	Rue Du Puits Croix Barb	24/03/1915	27/03/1915
Heading	War Diary of 1/9th Gurkha Rifles From 28th March 1915 & 30th April 1915		
War Diary	Rue Du Puits Croix Barbee	28/03/1915	29/03/1915
War Diary	Trenches Subsection B Southern Section	29/03/1915	31/03/1915
War Diary	Vielle Chapelle	01/04/1915	09/04/1915
War Diary	Croix Marmuse	10/04/1915	11/04/1915
War Diary	In Front Of Neuve Chapelle Subsection D	12/04/1915	23/04/1915
War Diary	Trenches Neuve Chapelle Sub Section D	24/04/1915	27/04/1915
War Diary	A. 1 Redoubt	28/04/1915	30/04/1915
Heading	War Diary of 1st Battalion 9th Gurkha Rifles. From 1st May 1915 To 31st May 1915.		
Miscellaneous	From Officer Commanding 1/9th Gurkhas Rifles	06/06/1915	06/06/1915

War Diary	Lansdowne Port (a1)	01/05/1915	03/05/1915
War Diary	Vielle Chapelle	04/05/1915	09/05/1915
War Diary	Rue De Bois	09/05/1915	09/05/1915
War Diary	Vielle Chapelle	10/05/1915	19/05/1915
War Diary	Croix Barbee	20/05/1915	21/05/1915
War Diary	Vielle Chapelle	22/05/1915	24/05/1915
War Diary	Trenches Rue De Bois	25/05/1915	28/05/1915
War Diary	Albert Row	28/05/1915	31/05/1915
Heading	War Diary of 1/9th Gurkha Rifles From 1st June 1915 To 30th June 1915		
War Diary	Trenches R3-Q7	01/06/1915	03/06/1915
War Diary	King George Road	04/06/1915	07/06/1915
War Diary	Billets Vielle Chapelle	08/06/1915	16/06/1915
War Diary	Vielle Chapelle	17/06/1915	21/06/1915
War Diary	Kings Road	21/06/1915	24/06/1915
War Diary	Sub Section A Rue De Bois	25/06/1915	25/06/1915
War Diary	Before Down	26/06/1915	28/06/1915
War Diary	Princes Road R Subsection	29/06/1915	30/06/1915
Heading	War Diary of 1/9th Gurkha Rifles From 1st July 1915 To 31st July 1915		
War Diary	King's Road	01/07/1915	03/07/1915
War Diary	Midnights H.Q C Sub Section Rue De Bois.	03/07/1915	07/07/1915
War Diary	King George's Road	08/07/1915	11/07/1915
War Diary	St Floris	11/07/1915	31/07/1915
Heading	War Diary of 1st Battalion 9th Gurkha Rifles From 1st August 1915 To 31st August 1915		
War Diary	St Floris	01/08/1915	01/08/1915
War Diary	La Gorgue	02/08/1915	10/08/1915
War Diary	B Subsection Rue Tilleloy.	11/08/1915	13/08/1915
War Diary	Pont Du Hem	14/08/1915	17/08/1915
War Diary	Ebenezer Farm H.a A Sub Section	18/08/1915	20/08/1915
War Diary	Pont Due Stem	21/06/1915	25/06/1915
War Diary	La. Gorgue	26/08/1915	27/08/1915
War Diary	Square L 26	28/08/1915	29/08/1915
War Diary	Rugby Road	30/08/1915	31/08/1915
Heading	War Diary of 1st Battalion 9th Gurkha Rifles From 1st September 1915 To 30th September 1915		
War Diary	Rugby Road	01/09/1915	04/09/1915
War Diary	Cuthbert House	05/09/1915	11/09/1915
War Diary	Conduit Street Ind 5. B	12/09/1915	16/09/1915
War Diary	La Gorgue	17/09/1915	18/09/1915
War Diary	Cuthbert House Ind 5.B.	19/09/1915	30/09/1915
Heading	War Diary of 1/9th Gurkha Rifles From 1st October 1915 To 31st October 1915		
War Diary	Vielle Chapelle	01/10/1915	03/10/1915
War Diary	H. Qs Ind II C	03/10/1915	10/10/1915
War Diary	H.Qs. Bre Reserve	11/10/1915	14/10/1915
War Diary	Estaminet Comer	14/10/1915	21/10/1915
War Diary	Edward Road	21/10/1915	24/10/1915
War Diary	Paradis R.19.	25/10/1915	31/10/1915
Heading	War Diary of 1/9th Gurkha Rifles From 1st November 1915 To 30th November 1915		
War Diary	Paradis-R 19	01/11/1915	02/11/1915
War Diary	R34 Crd	03/11/1915	04/11/1915
War Diary	Rue De Berceaux	05/11/1915	06/11/1915
War Diary	Le Go Hasard	07/11/1915	13/11/1915

War Diary	Lieres	14/11/1915	18/11/1915
War Diary	Leshermaines	20/11/1915	30/11/1915

WO95/3941/3

1/9 Battalion Gurkha Rifles

MEERUT DIVISION
(9 DEHRA DUN BRIGADE

1-9TH GURKHA RIFLES
~~JAN - NOV 1915~~

1914 AUG - 1915 NOV

To MESOPOTAMIA

3 LAHORE DIV
9 GR

Meerut Division Aug-Dec 1914
1/9th Gurkha Rifles.

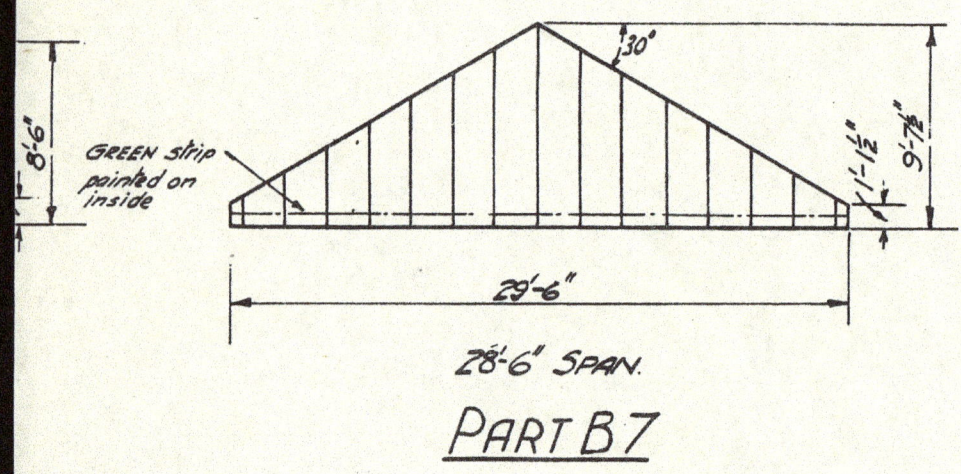

28'-6" SPAN.

PART B7

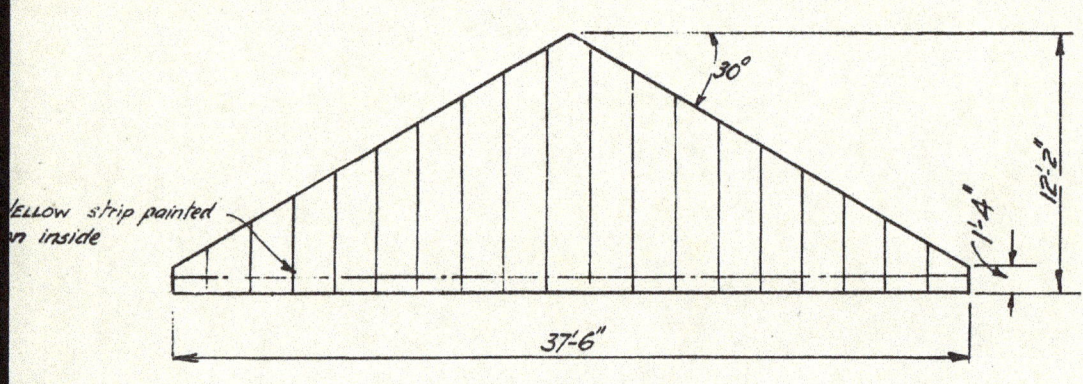

36'-6" SPAN

PART B8

SETS OF EXTERNAL GABLE SHEETING

WHEN FIXED

fixed they conform to the dimensions shown.
be clearly marked by means of a 6" coloured
indicated
x 24 gauge, & to be laid with single side laps.

AMENDED 19-10-38.

SHEETS. DRAWING No. H. 356/37

Dehra Dun
Recruit

War Diary
1/9th Gurkha Rifles
from 9/6/14 to 27·10·14
August
Volume I

Army Form C. 2118.

WAR DIARY
or
INTELLIGENCE-SUMMARY.

(Erase heading not required.)

Instructions regarding War Diaries and Intelligence Summaries are contained in F. S. Regs., Part II, and the Staff Manual respectively. Title pages will be prepared in manuscript.

Hour, Date, Place.	Summary of Events and Information.	Remarks and references to Appendices
6. am. 9th Aug. 1914 Dehra Dun	Orders received by wire to mobilize.	As overleaf. See Appendix. A.
9. am. 31st Aug. 1914	Orders received to concentrate.	
1st Sept "	The Battalion left Dehra in 2 troop trains leaving at 9.35 am and 2.45 pm. The two trains were joined up at LAKHSAR.	For strength of Batn See Appendix. A.
9.15 am Friday 4th Sept. BOMBAY.	Arrived at his Alexandra Docks, Bombay. Here were accommodated in a large goods shed at his CARNAC BANDAR.	Details, see Appendix A.
9.0 am Monday 14th Sept.	Embarked by half Battalions in S.S. ANGORA and S.S. ARANKOLA.	Details see Appendix A.
11. am 16th Sept.	Left his docks and anchored in the Stream.	
12. noon 20th Sept.	Flotilla left Bombay under escort of H.M.S. Swiftsure, H.M.S. Fox and R.I.M.S. DUFFERIN.	
23rd Sept.	Met transports from KARACHI with H.M.S DARTMOUTH and R.I.M.S. HARDING. H.M.S. DARTMOUTH and H.M.S. FOX left with 2 ships for B.E.AFRICA	

Gulab Singh & Sons, Calcutta—No. 22 Army C.—5-8-14—1,07,000.

Army Form C. 2118.

WAR DIARY
or
INTELLIGENCE SUMMARY.

(Erase heading not required.)

Instructions regarding War Diaries and Intelligence Summaries are contained in F. S. Regs., Part II, and the Staff Manual respectively. Title pages will be prepared in manuscript.

Hour, Date, Place.	Summary of Events and Information.	Remarks and references to Appendices
11 p.m. 26th Sept. 27th Sept. 1914	Death of one Rifleman reported on S.S. ARANCOLA from enteric. Passed Aden.	
9 a.m. 28th "	Passed PERIM ISLAND.	
9 p.m. 29th "	Went on ahead of convoy for SUEZ.	
5.30 p.m. 2nd OCTOBER	Arrived at SUEZ. Received marine orders.	
10.0 a.m. 3rd "	Left SUEZ. Pickets of H.L.I. and 4th Gurkhas manning the canal. Weather very fine and much cooler. Arrived at ISMAILIA at 3 p.m. anchored to allow battleship to pass.	
	Left Ismailia at about 4.45 p.m.	
	Arrived PORT SAID at 11.45 p.m. Harri camp of H.L.I. 1 and 4 G.R. and 125 Rifles at ISMAILIA.	
PORT SAID 4th OCTOBER	Anchored in Port Said Harbour. Lt. Colonel Widdicombe took over command of the Battalion.	
11.30 a.m. 5th OCTOBER	Worked out with steam.	

Army Form C. 2118.

WAR DIARY
INTELLIGENCE SUMMARY.
(Erase heading not required.)

Instructions regarding War Diaries and Intelligence Summaries are contained in F. S. Regs., Part II, and the Staff Manual respectively. Title pages will be prepared in manuscript.

Hour, Date, Place.	Summary of Events and Information.	Remarks and references to Appendices
PORT SAID 2.15 pm 6th OCTOBER.	hove 3 miles further out into the stream.	
4.45 pm "	left PORT SAID for MARSEILLES. Weather very fine.	
AT SEA 8th OCTOBER.	Strong wind blowing – fairly rough. being high in the night – men sick.	
9th " "	Sea has gone down.	
10th " "	Passed MALTA at 8. am.	
11th " "	Passed SARDINIA at about 11. am.	
MARSEILLES 12th "	Arrived MARSEILLES at 7.15 am. Disembarked and formed up in large shed at 8.30 am – armed with M.III rifle. Ammn. was also changed. MKVII Ammn being issued.	
	Half the battalion left the docks at 2.45 pm. Half the battalion was left at the docks for fatigue work.	
	Marched to about 10 miles through MARSEILLES to Camp GALEHTTNE, arrived at about 5.30 pm. Transport started arriving in about 3/4 hour later.	
CAMP GALEHTTNE MARSEILLES 13th OCT "	Half Batln marched in about 12.30 am. weather fine. Heavy dew at night.	

Army Form C. 2118.

WAR DIARY
or
INTELLIGENCE SUMMARY.

(Erase heading not required.)

Instructions regarding War Diaries and Intelligence Summaries are contained in F. S. Regs., Part II, and the Staff Manual respectively. Title pages will be prepared in manuscript.

Hour, Date, Place.	Summary of Events and Information.	Remarks and references to Appendices
Camp BARENTINE MARSEILLES.		
14th OCT. 1914.	Heavy rain.	
15th OCT.	Heavy rain during most of day and night.	
16th OCT.	Heavy rain during night. Received orders to entrain tomorrow at 6.5 p.m.	
17th OCT.	Entrained at GARE D'ARENC at 6.5 p.m. for ORLEANS.	
18th OCT.	Travelling. Long halt at TOULOUSE.	Strength of Battn etc. see Appendix A
19th OCT.	" Long halt at ARGENTENS.	
ORLEANS.		
20th OCT.	Arrived at ORLEANS at 2 a.m.; marched to camp.	
21st OCT.	Halt. Arranged for warm clothing for men and followers.	
22nd OCT.	An airplane passed over the camp at about 4.45 p.m.	
23rd OCT.	Marched to LA CIRCOTTE rifle range. Each man to find with his new rifle. Was heavy marching order. Divisional Route March.	
24th OCT.		
25th OCT.	Surplus kit sent back to Marseilles. All civil public and private to be struck and handed over at 5 p.m. All private lines have been taken over by government.	

1/9 GR

Army Form C. 2118.

WAR DIARY
or
INTELLIGENCE SUMMARY.
(Erase heading not required.)

Instructions regarding War Diaries and Intelligence Summaries are contained in F. S. Regs., Part II, and the Staff Manual respectively. Title pages will be prepared in manuscript.

Hour, Date, Place.		Summary of Events and Information.	Remarks and references to Appendices
ORLEANS.			
25th Oct. 1914	2.1 pm	Received orders to entrain uniforms at 2.5 pm.	JRA.
26th Oct.	8.15 am	Tents struck and handed over.	
	1.15 pm	Battalion paraded and marched to Station.	
	2.5 pm	Started to entrain carts, wagons, watercarts etc with kit ready loaded on lines.	
On Train.	4 pm	Entraining completed.	
27th Oct.	1.35 pm	Reached ABBEVILLE.	JRA.
	4.35 pm	" ETAPLES.	
	8 pm	" CALAIS.	
	11 pm	" HAZEBROUCK.	
	2.30 am	" MERVILLE. Detrained and marched to billet	JRA.
MERVILLE.	6.15 am	in School of Institution N.D. D'ESPERANCE. Transport came in.	Strength of Baton on arrival at MERVILLE See APPENDIX A

Gulab Singh & Sons, Calcutta—No. 22 Army C.—5-8-14—1,07,000.

1/9 GOORKHAS.

WAR DIARY
or
INTELLIGENCE SUMMARY.

(Erase heading not required.)

APPENDIX. A.

Army Form C. 2118.

Instructions regarding War Diaries and Intelligence Summaries are contained in F. S. Regs., Part II, and the Staff Manual respectively. Title pages will be prepared in manuscript.

Hour, Date, Place.	Summary of Events and Information.	Remarks and references to Appendices
1.	The mobilization of the Battalion was carried out satisfactorily, but owing to its two' season," was considerably under strength; and a large draft had to be taken from the 2nd Battalion viz:— British officers 2 Subedars 1 Jemadars 3 havildars 7 Naicks 9 Buglers 1 Riflemen 99 and orders having been received to take a first reinforcement of 1 G.O, 2 havildars and 30 rifles, a further draft was accordingly taken from the 2nd Battalion.	
2.	It was understood by us and by 1st Brigade that our equipping station was at ROORKEE. This was not so as it was at MEERUT. considerable delay was caused by this alone as F.S. clothing and compressed fodder was not immediately available.	

Army Form C. 2118.

WAR DIARY
or
INTELLIGENCE SUMMARY.

Appendix A (cont).

(Erase heading not required.)

Instructions regarding War Diaries and Intelligence Summaries are contained in F. S. Regs., Part II, and the Staff Manual respectively. Title pages will be prepared in manuscript.

Hour, Date, Place.	Summary of Events and Information.	Remarks and references to Appendices
3.	Strength of Battalion on leaving DEHRA DUN BRITISH OFFICERS. 9 ⊕ ✠ GOORKHA OFFICERS. 17 and 1. S.A.S N.C.O's and MEN. 804 ⊕✠ 　　　　　　　　　 1 I.R.M. GOORKHA OFFICERS)　　　 Rifle men　　　　) 3 No 7. Ammunition Column. 　　　　　　　　 ――― TOTAL NATIVE RANKS. 826 F.S. slings&c　　　　 753　 FOLLOWERS 1st reinforcements　　 73　 Public 2. 　　　　　　　 ――― Private. 18. 　　　　　　　　 826	✠ Inclusive 1 G.O 2 Harrisons 70 Rifles 1st Reinforcements. ⊕ Exclusive of Major Bignell. D.A.D of Railway Transport Lt Col Widdicombe ⎫ Major Hogg　　　　⎬ will Capt Pike　　　　　⎭ meet Battn 　　　　　　　　　 at Port SAID
4.	The Battalion was put up in a large godown at his CANNAC BANDAR with his 2nd K.E.O. Goorkhas. The arrangements made were most satisfactory and his been very comfortable. This was to have been his weather was extremely bad.	

1/9th G.R.

Appendix A.

Army Form C. 2118.

WAR DIARY
or
INTELLIGENCE SUMMARY.

(Erase heading not required.)

Instructions regarding War Diaries and Intelligence Summaries are contained in F. S. Regs., Part II, and the Staff Manual respectively. Title pages will be prepared in manuscript.

Hour, Date, Place.	Summary of Events and Information.	Remarks and references to Appendices
5.	The battalion embarked † by ½ Battalions in the S.S. ANGORA and S.S. ARANCOLA as follows. S.S. ANGORA (with 2-2 K.E.O. Goorkhas under COLONEL NORIE D.S.O.) Capt Mackinnon Comdg 1/9 G.R. Nos. 2 and 4 D. Coys. and march from detachment STRENGTH: B.Os. .... 5 ⊙ G.Os. .... 9 and 1.S.O.S N.C.Os and men .... 400 Followers .... 22 Horses .... 7 Mules .... 38 Transport personnel . 13 S.S. ARANCOLA (with 6th JATS) ⊘ Capt Hurley Commdg Wing 1/9 GR Nos. 1 and 3. Coys STRENGTH: B.Os. 4 ⊘ G.Os. .... 8 N.C.Os and men .. 400 Followers .... 23 Horses ...... 6 Mules .... 37 Transport personnel 18	† Strength as before less 4 riflemen 2 sick men 2 sick attendants Left in 2n Rajput hospital Sick in lie autre (believe) ⊙ Capt Mackinnon Comdg „ Shepherd Adjt „ Lt Waller Q.M. „ Hurvey „ Ingester ⊘ Capt Hurley Comdg Lt Bailie 2Lt Kemp Lt Col Daly, I.M.S.

Army Form C. 2118.

1/9. G.R.
WAR DIARY
or
INTELLIGENCE SUMMARY. APPENDIX A.
(Erase heading not required.)

Instructions regarding War Diaries and Intelligence Summaries are contained in F. S. Regs., Part II, and the Staff Manual respectively. Title pages will be prepared in manuscript.

Hour, Date, Place.		Summary of Events and Information.	Remarks and references to Appendices
ENTRAINMENT AT MARSEILLES. 17th OCT.	1.	Struck tents at 8 a.m. Transport – 11 lorries (carts) loaded up by 11 am and proceeded to No 2. Print under escort of B. coy (Col. Haviland) and commanded by Lt. POYNDER to GARE D'ARENC. The Battalion marched at 12 noon strength as under. B.Os. 12. G.Os. 16 N.C.Os & men 737 Followers 44 + 14 Draught personnel mules 46 Chargers 13 A.T. carts 9 arrived at GARE D'ARENC at 2.45 pm. Advance party under Lt. Walton had gone on ahead and marked out trains. Loaded up two trains and completed entrainment by 6 pm. Left GARE D'ARENC at 9.5 pm. arrived at ORANGE at 8 am 2½ hours halt	

1/9 GR

Appendix A.

Army Form C. 2118.
5

WAR DIARY
or
INTELLIGENCE SUMMARY.
(Erase heading not required.)

Instructions regarding War Diaries and Intelligence Summaries are contained in F.S. Regs., Part II, and the Staff Manual respectively. Title pages will be prepared in manuscript.

Hour, Date, Place.	Summary of Events and Information.	Remarks and references to Appendices
18th OCT.	Men got hot coffee. N.C.O.'s and G.O.'s whisky. TOULOUSE. 5 p.m. – 3 hours halt – men cooked their food.	
19th OCT.	Long halt at ARGENTENS – 3 hours halt – men cooked and were given hot coffee. All arrangements excellent – and railway and military officials very obliging. Arrived at ORLEANS at 2 p.m. 2. am. Detrained and marched to camp (1½ miles) leaving one whole company to unload kit. Train.	
20th OCT.		
24th OCT.	For divisional Route march G.O.'s, N.C.O.'s and men were issued the following in addition to ordinary field service scale. On the man. 1 warm vest – 1 flannel shirt – 1 warm drawers. Carrier by man. 1 great coat – 1 blanket – 1 sweater. 1 Balaclava cap – 1 tin food. In F.S. kit. 1 waterproof sheet – 1 blanket – 1 towel – 1 piece of soap – 1 leg bands.	

Army Form C. 2118.

WAR DIARY
or
INTELLIGENCE SUMMARY.   APPENDIX. A.

(Erase heading not required.)

Instructions regarding War Diaries and Intelligence Summaries are contained in F. S. Regs., Part II, and the Staff Manual respectively. Title pages will be prepared in manuscript.

Hour, Date, Place.	Summary of Events and Information.	Remarks and references to Appendices
X	Strength of Battalion on arrival at MERVILLE	X Names.
	B.O's 10.	Col. Hiedicombe Cmdg.
	G.O's 15	Major Hogg 2nd in command
	N.C.O's and men 728.	Capt Mackinnon. No. 3 coy
	Followers 41.	Capt PIKE. No. 4 coy
	Transport Personnel. 14	" Hudson No. 2 coy
	A.S.C. Drivers 7	" Hoyland Adjt.
	Mules 46	" Wallin H.Q. officer
	A.T. carts 9	" Munro Quarter Master
	Chargers 15.	" Bailie Sig. officer
	Horses 18	" Prynder Transport Officer
	Water carts 2	
	Cook cart 1	Major Pigott appt'd DADRT
	G.S. Waggons 6	under I.G.C. permanent
	Bicycles 9	Lt Kemp temporarily attached as R.T.O
	Interpreters 3	
O		O. 2/Lt DOLL
	3 men detached at present to act as Orderlies	Lt ROUBINY
	6 men transferred to No 128 Ind. Field Ambulance	" DNAN
	1 Sounder Labadeen " "	

121/4046

WAR DIARY
of
1/9th Gurkha Rifles
From 28-10-14 To 12-1-15

Army Form C. 2118.

1/9th G.R.

WAR DIARY
or
INTELLIGENCE SUMMARY.

(Erase heading not required.)

Hour, Date, Place.	Summary of Events and Information.	Remarks and references to Appendices
MERVILLE. 28th OCT. 12. MIDNIGHT.	Received orders to march to VIELLE CHAPELLE distant about 6 miles.	
29th OCT. 9.45 am.	Marched from MERVILLE at 9.45 am.	
VIELLE CHAPELLE. 2. p.m.	Arrived in VIELLE CHAPELLE and went into billets.	
7.30 pm.	Received orders to march at 11 pm to relieve certain regiments in the trenches.	
10.45 p.m.	Marched at 10.45 pm behind the 2nd G.R. and 6th JATS. To relieve certain regiments of his 3rd Div. in the trenches 19th Ind. Infantry Bde detailed to hold from the cross roads exclusive on main LA BASSEE – ESTAIRES road, inclusive towards CHAPIGNY. The Bde took up positions in following order from the right. SEAFORTHS – 6th JATS – 9th GOORKHAS – 2nd GOORKHAS Battalion marched carrying 200 rds a man – entrenching tools – waterproof sheet – blanket – sweater – waistcoat – field and 1 day's ration. 2nd and 9th G.R. under orders of Col. NORIE D.S.O. marched to ROUGE CROIX village.	
30th OCT. 2.45 a.m.	Arrived at PONT LOGY about 1 mile beyond ROUGE CROIX. Turned down the road from PONT LOGY, which runs behind his trenches, to take up positions as follows – from the right No 1, 2, 3, 4. Double companies under Capt. PIKE, MURRAY MAJOR HOGG and Capt MACKINNON respectively. Having paired down his packs about midnight, a fairly heavy rifle fire was opened on the trenches by his Germans. Luckily all his shots went high, but 2 men and 1 was hit gun mules were hit.	No. 3071. Rn NARBIR GHARTI, Atg. hit in his thigh. No. 3198. Rn PADAM SING MAHAT. N.Eng. hit in knee.

1/9th G.R.

Army Form C. 2118.

WAR DIARY
or
INTELLIGENCE SUMMARY.
(Erase heading not required.)

Instructions regarding War Diaries and Intelligence Summaries are contained in F.S. Regs., Part II, and the Staff Manual respectively. Title pages will be prepared in manuscript.

Hour, Date, Place.	Summary of Events and Information.	Remarks and references to Appendices
N. W. of NEUVE CHAPELLE. 4. am	been behaved very well under trying circumstances. It was dark, we didn't know where the trenches were, and although the enemies fire was not heavy, our own troops in the trenches were firing very heavily, and the noise was terrific. Our guns fired pretty frequently. Most of the double companies were settled in their trenches, having relieved the Royal Scots and LINCOLNS. After one or two short outbursts of fire towards dawn, everything remained quiet.	Killed No 2711. Rm. Mantir Ghurti H 2941 "Satabahadur hal H 2649 MANBIR SAHI H. 2-9 Wounded 2572 Budimon Roka H 3134 Lalbahadur Sahi H 2052 Gori Lal H
30th OCT.	All quiet until about 3. pm when the Germans started bombarding the trenches with shrapnel. They got the range of our trenches on the left exactery, killing 3 men and knocking over the maxim gun, also damaging the trenches and breaking down the parapet, exposing the men to machine gun fire, by which 3 men were wounded. As soon as it was dark, stretchers were sent out and wounded were brought in. Ration parties were sent back beyond ROUGE CROIX. Also and water replenished. The germans opened fire intermittently through the night. No damage done.	

Gulab Singh & Sons, Calcutta—No. 22 Army C.—5-8-14—1,07,000.

1/9 G.R. 8

Army Form C. 2118.

WAR DIARY
or
INTELLIGENCE SUMMARY.

(Erase heading not required.)

Hour, Date, Place.	Summary of Events and Information.	Remarks and references to Appendices
TRENCHES PONT LOGY. 31st OCT.	Germans started shelling trenches at 6.30 a.m. and continued until dark. No damage done except on extreme left of No 4. coy. where range the German guns had got exactly. 6 men of H. Coy. wounded – no other casualties in Baln. Several aeroplanes seen during the day. Trenches strengthened during the night, and barbed wire sent up to place in front of trenches.	Wounded by Shell fire. No 2978. Khim lal Khatri. H. Coy. 2575 Tekbahadur " 2817 Dhanbahadur Sahi 2824 Khambahadur " 3086 Bhakta Sing Thapa 2984 Ranbir "
1st Nov. 9 a.m.	A few german shells came over trenches. 2 allies aeroplanes sailed along german lines at about) am being heavily bombarded by german guns, and although the puffs of shrapnel shewing shrapnel bursts, were all about them, neither of them was hit. The whole day the trenches especially No 4 coy were heavily shelled.	
2nd Nov.	News came in that the left double company of the 2nd G.R. had been blown out of their trenches by mortars.	

Army Form C. 2118.

9

1/9 G.R.

WAR DIARY
or
INTELLIGENCE SUMMARY.

(Erase heading not required.)

Instructions regarding War Diaries and Intelligence Summaries are contained in F. S. Regs., Part II, and the Staff Manual respectively. Title pages will be prepared in manuscript.

Hour, Date, Place.	Summary of Events and Information.	Remarks and references to Appendices
TRENCHES. PONTLOGY. 2nd Nov. 10 am	Sent message to Bde. stating that the left of the 2nd GR had had to evacuate their trenches and asking for support.	
11 am	1 Squadron of 7th D.G's. 1 " " Poonah Horse 1 D.C. of 6th JATS. Came up in support. About 150 of 2nd GR (1 Sqdt Poonah horse and a weak Coy of 9th GR (2 Platoons) under Lt BAILLIE and KEMP started off in the direction of the right of 2nd GR trenches to endeavour to regain their - under orders of Col MORIE, D.S.O. They came under a very heavy shrapnel and machine gun fire. Lt BAILLIE and 2 men of F coy. were killed. LT BAILLIE leading F coy under a heavy fire with conspicuous gallantry. The party of 2nd GR had several casualties, and Lt Poonah horse lost being heavily, Col. SWANSTON their Colonel being killed went in the whole day. heavy shelling	

Army Form C. 2118.

10

WAR DIARY
or
INTELLIGENCE SUMMARY.

1/9. G.R.

(Erase heading not required.)

Hour, Date, Place.	Summary of Events and Information.	Remarks and references to Appendices
TRENCHES, PONT LOGY Nov. 2nd about 5.30 pm.	Col. NORIE, D.S.O. collected about 80 of 2nd G.R., Double Coy of 6th JATS and a Coy of Royal Scots and endeavoured to make a second attempt to regain the trenches. They got close up to lost trenches but came under a heavy maxim gun fire, and lines being no support, had to retire.	
7. pm.	2 Battns came up. Royal Scots and a composite batn of 34th PIONEERS - 58th Rifles - 9th BHOPALS. Line of trenches joined up with Connaught, about 400 x behind his 2nd GR trenches. The 4th B. Coy endeavoured to swing back their left flank by digging a new trench, but whilst digging came under heavy maxim gun fire and had to lie down. Trench was too shallow not to be able to have him deep enough by daylight. As 34th Pioneers were behind us. filled up old trench and brought 4th Coy back to Helgrs as reserve.	
Nov. 3rd 8. am.	Germans commenced shelling trenches. Quieted down. Two french batteries came up behind us.	

Army Form C. 2118.

1/9 GR

WAR DIARY
or
INTELLIGENCE SUMMARY.
(Erase heading not required.)

Hour, Date, Place.	Summary of Events and Information.	Remarks and references to Appendices
PONT LOGY TRENCHES.		
Nov. 3rd 11.30 am	Fixed up communication with O.C. French Battery.	
11.50 am	Heavy firing all along the line, but no known attack on our trenches. All quiet. Sent small parties of scouts out, who said they had seen enemy wearing Gtackwa caps and British coats however.	
Nov. 4th 12.0 n.n.	O.C. French battery sent up asking us to thin for him. Results were disastrous, this second since dropping all round our trenches. Luckily no damage done. All quiet during the afternoon on our part of the line, but heavy firing near 6th JATS. and SEAFORTHS.	
6.30 pm	An officer from the Royal Scots came and told us of a counter attack that is to be carried out tonight. Last night the Germans had apparently occupied an abandoned trench of the Connaughts, which they had neglected to fill up when moving back their right flank	

1/9 G.R.

WAR DIARY
or
INTELLIGENCE SUMMARY.
(Erase heading not required.)

Army Form C. 2118.

Hour, Date, Place.	Summary of Events and Information.	Remarks and references to Appendices
PONT LOGY TRENCHES Nov. 4th (Cont).	1 Coy of Royal Scots were to take up a position in clump of high trees on our left. At 12 midnight they were to commence a heavy fire to draw the Germans towards it. At the same time a company of the connaughts were to charge the trench and try to fill it up. Our guns bombarding the enemies supports meanwhile.	
1.a.m	Our guns firing. Some of our shells dropped in our trenches, killing me and wounding 6 men. 2 men wounded in No. 1 coy.	
Nov. 5th 9.30 a.m.	Germans commenced shelling our second line. Reports from scouts of No 2 that the enemy had got an advanced trench about 200' from their front line, with 2 machine guns. Informed the gunners.	
2.45 p.m.	Shelling continued, getting very hot at about 2.45 pm when a heavy rifle fire started in front of 3rd Coy. A body of gurkhas came out of their trench about 200' from ours. They immediately came under a very heavy rifle fire from our No 3 coy trenches	

1/9 G.R.

Army Form C. 2118.

WAR DIARY
or
INTELLIGENCE SUMMARY.
(Erase heading not required.)

Instructions regarding War Diaries and Intelligence Summaries are contained in F.S. Regs., Part II, and the Staff Manual respectively. Title pages will be prepared in manuscript.

Hour, Date, Place.	Summary of Events and Information.	Remarks and references to Appendices
PONT LOGY TRENCHES. Nov. 5th (cont)	Most of them ran back into their trench, about 30 however came on. They were all knocked over, our gunners getting within 10 yards of our trench, then very pluckily returned with themselves. Had No 3 Hill been free, many more Germans would have been accounted for. Firing died down and quiet for rest of day. Got 2 Helmets and 3 German rifles. As soon as it was dark G Coy went out to inform new trench on left of our trenches. A heavy fire opened by Germans with machine guns. Our guns did very good work in front of No 2 and 3 coys.	
11.30 pm	Germans opened a heavy fire. Germans evidently becoming time dead.	
Nov. 6th 6. a.m.	A very misty morning. Found that the Germans were holding a trench between 100x of No 3 and H coy trenches.	

13

Army Form C. 2118.

1/9 GR

14

WAR DIARY
or
INTELLIGENCE SUMMARY.

(Erase heading not required.)

Instructions regarding War Diaries and Intelligence Summaries are contained in F. S. Regs., Part II, and the Staff Manual respectively. Title pages will be prepared in manuscript.

Hour, Date, Place.	Summary of Events and Information.	Remarks and references to Appendices
Nov. 6th (cont).	Got the gunner officer up to the trenches, to have a look. He put some hydritic shells into the german trench which stopped them digging. Being mid-day the which day heavy rifle fire started and two germans just some shrapnel over No 1 coy. Two men wounded. Quiet nearly the whole night, except for one or two slight outbreaks of fire. being misty and cold	
Nov. 7th 8.45 am	Germans started shelling near the JATS. Enemy again entrenching near No. 3. coy.	
10. am	A heavy rifle and gun fire opened on us by Germans which gradually died down. Message received up from Brigade telling us to keep in close touch with german trenches when apparently opened to ascertain if being were still held. Message received from Hogg to say that WALTON had been shot dead, whilst surrounding his of his machine guns.	

1/9 GR

WAR DIARY
or
INTELLIGENCE SUMMARY.

Army Form C. 2118.
15

(Erase heading not required.)

Instructions regarding War Diaries and Intelligence Summaries are contained in F. S. Regs., Part II, and the Staff Manual respectively. Title pages will be prepared in manuscript.

Hour, Date, Place.	Summary of Events and Information.	Remarks and references to Appendices
Nov. 7th (continued).	Being heavily shelled during the afternoon. Supper truck of No 2 hit by a Jack Johnson. 6 men killed and about 10 wounded. About 8.30 pm a heavy rifle fire started by enemy, but replied to by our men. Shell fire employed by germans after dark. Up to present date, germans have never shelled us after dark.	
12 midnight	50 men of 7th D.Gs. came up as reserve.	
6.30 am	7th D.G. left.	
Nov. 8th	Quiet nearly the whole day.	
6 pm	Germans started shelling the head running behind us from PONT LOGY.	
Nov. 9th 6 am	Decided to change pit of head quarters to large farm house on other side of road, as being seen to know we have got (artillery) Signalling station at present the Gro. Had not been in view the Gro. have been an	

WAR DIARY or INTELLIGENCE SUMMARY

Army Form C. 2118.
1/9 GR
16

Hour, Date, Place.	Summary of Events and Information.	Remarks and references to Appendices
Nov 9th continued	hour, when the town was very heavily shelled and we had to make a hurried exit — going back to our old Hd Qrs. Support trenches very heavily shelled, mortar also opened fire, but did no damage except to fill up communication trench. 6 men wounded in our reserve trench. Reports from Cry Staff that West Gurwana have occupied advance trenches leaving his right hand grenade were horm also my trenches. They are sapping up to his apex of No 3 Cry trench into No 4 Cry trench. Shelling continued. Gurwana in front of No. 2 Cry are about 80' from No 1 lining a hedge (ditch). This should have been cut down.	
5.30 hrs	1 Cry of 2nd GR under Lt Stowes came up as reserve	

1/9 GR

Army Form C. 2118.

WAR DIARY
or
INTELLIGENCE SUMMARY.

(Erase heading not required.)

Instructions regarding War Diaries and Intelligence Summaries are contained in F. S. Regs., Part II, and the Staff Manual respectively. Title pages will be prepared in manuscript.

Hour, Date, Place.	Summary of Events and Information.	Remarks and references to Appendices
Nov. 9th contd.	Put him on to dig 2 short lengths of fire trench behind No 2 and 3 coys.	
Nov 10th	A very quiet night. Being quiet in his turning. Enemy reported in high clumps of trees to our left. Had them shelled.	
11.30 am	Bombarded enemies trenches and NEUVE CHAPELLE. No result so far as could be seen.	
3 pm	Col. NORIE. D.S.O came to the or to say that he had 1 coy and 1 coy of 7 D.G.s about 400" behind HQ. 2 GR	
12 midnight	Our guns again bombarded enemies trenches endeavouring to destroy iron house in front of Scots line. Holiday was hit 1st army West Gurwans had hit shields. All quiet during night.	

1/9 GR

WAR DIARY
or
INTELLIGENCE SUMMARY.

Army Form C. 2118
18 7

Instructions regarding War Diaries and Intelligence Summaries are contained in F. S. Regs., Part II, and the Staff Manual respectively. Title pages will be prepared in manuscript.

(Erase heading not required.)

Hour, Date, Place.	Summary of Events and Information.	Remarks and references to Appendices.
PONT LOGY TRENCHES. Nov. 11th.	Received orders that we would be relieved by Suffolk Regiment on night 12/13th.	Lt. BERRY joined Batt on 12th. Lt MURRAY slightly wounded on 11th.
Nov. 12th 2. p.m.	Colonel and Adjutant of Suffolks came up to see about relief.	
8.30 p.m.	Suffolks came up and commenced relieving our Company by company from his left.	
12. midnight	Relief completed. Colonel Batn at ROUGE CROIX and marched to Billets at VIEILLE CHAPELLE	
Nov. 13. 3. am.	Reached billets at VIEILLE CHAPELLE	
12. noon.	Received orders to march at 5.pm to RICHEBOURG L'AVOUE to act as reserve to GARHWAL BDE. distance about 5½ miles.	
5. pm.	marched.	
7.30 pm.	Reached GARHWAL BDE Hd Qrs.	
12.0 midnight	Received orders to send 1 coy. to gap between 1 and 2nd 39 GARHWALIS No.10.C under Capt PIKE and with Lt POYNDER stand at	
Nov. 14. 12.30 am	Received orders to march remainder of Batn up.	

Army Form C. 2118
No 19

WAR DIARY 1/9 G.R.
or
INTELLIGENCE SUMMARY.
(Erase heading not required.)

Instructions regarding War Diaries and Intelligence Summaries are contained in F. S. Regs., Part II, and the Staff Manual respectively. Title pages will be prepared in manuscript.

Hour, Date, Place.	Summary of Events and Information.	Remarks and references to Appendices.
Nov. 14. 3. a.m.	Received orders to take up position of readiness in 2-3 G.R. trenches.	
10. a.m.	Received orders to return to billets in VIEILLE CHAPELLE	
Nov. 15. VIEILLE CHAPELLE. 9. a.m.	Received orders to go into billets at CSE du RAUX near LE TOURRET, marching at 9. a.m. on 16th	
Nov. 16.	1 Hav. and 2 riflemen, sent to form portion of guard of honor at funeral of LORD ROBERTS. marched to LE TOURRET and there to billets at LOISNE. Attached to and came under orders of 20th Bde (GARHWR) Received orders that evening to send ½ Battn that night to billets in Rue de LEPINETTE. No 2 and 3 coys under Major HOGG left LOISNE for RUE de LEPINETTE. 1 Hav. and 2 riflemen again sent to form guard of honor on LORD ROBERTS remains, being afterwards assisted to carry the coffin to gun carriage. Jem Subahadur also detailed to attend LORD ROBERTS funeral.	LORD ROBERTS. Capt Heyland went to Hosp. with bad feet Lt. Poynder to act as Adjutant
Nov. 17.	marched Nos. 1 and 4 coys to billets in Rue de LEPINETTE joining remainder of Battn. later received orders to billet ½ Battn in Rue du BOIS, about ½ mile from RUE DE LEPINETTE.	

Army Form C. 2118

WAR DIARY 1/9 G.R.
or
INTELLIGENCE SUMMARY.

(Erase heading not required.)

Instructions regarding War Diaries and Intelligence Summaries are contained in F. S. Regs., Part II, and the Staff Manual respectively. Title pages will be prepared in manuscript.

page 20

Hour, Date, Place.	Summary of Events and Information.	Remarks and references to Appendices.
Nov. 17th 5. pm	Marched with Nos. 1 and 4 coys to new billets in Rue du Bois. No. 2 coy. under Lt. BERRY had to report to O.C. 1/39 Garhwal Rifles at RICHEBOURG L'AVOUE at 5. pm to dig trenches. 4 previously wounded men rejoined Batn.	
Nov. 18th 4. pm	Sent out parties under Capt PIKE to collect inhabitants in RUE du CAILLOUX and RUE de BERCEAUX, brought in some 60 persons of both sexes. Left with D Company commanders to look over 1/39 trenches at RICHEBOURG L'AVOUE, returning about 9. pm. Nos. 3 and 4 coys on working fatigues on 1/39, LEICESTER, and 2nd G.R. trenches, under CAPT MACKINNON and LT. BERRY.	Major BIGNELL joined Batn. and took over command of No 2 coy.
Nov. 19th	Other parties sent out to bring in inhabitants, from No 1 coy. No 2 coy. and 2 platoons No 4 coy. left at 5. pm. for RICHEBOURG L'AVOUE by unfrequented from trenches of 1/39 and proceeded to carrying out relief of 1/39 trenches.	

Army Form C. 2118.

WAR DIARY
or
INTELLIGENCE SUMMARY.

(Erase heading not required.)

Instructions regarding War Diaries and Intelligence Summaries are contained in F. S. Regs., Part II, and the Staff Manual respectively. Title pages will be prepared in manuscript.

Hour, Date, Place.	Summary of Events and Information.	Remarks and references to Appendices.
Nov. 19th	No 1 and 3 cays. and 2 platoons No 4 cay. and machine guns arriving an hour later, and similarly relieving 1/39 trenches.	
7.30pm	A fairly heavy fire commenced - enemy attempting but failing to rush picquet on left of 1/39 trench line.	
11.30pm	Relief completed. 2 previously wounded men rejoined.	
Nov. 20th	2 men G. in wounded last night by accidental explosion of rocket.	
3.1am	Sub. Major BIDANI SING ABIKHEI luckily wounded in the trenches, and died almost immediately after arrival at regimental first aid post. 1 man 3rd M.Cy. killed in trenches.	
Nov. 21st	Colonel Gunning and Adjt of 47th Sikhs arrived to look over trench line. Information received at midnight that his French expected an attack at GIVENCHY, all units warned to be on the look out.	Capt Hoyland rejoined from hospital.

WAR DIARY
or
INTELLIGENCE SUMMARY.

(Erase heading not required.)

Army Form C. 2118.

Hour, Date, Place.	Summary of Events and Information.	Remarks and references to Appendices.
RICHEBOURG L'AVOUE, TRENCHES		
Nov. 22"		
Nov. 23" 5.30 pm	Had 47th SIKHS and 1 coy 15th SIKHS arrived to relieve No 1 and 2 coys of the Batn.	
6.30 pm	Remainder of 47th SIKHS and 60 men of 15 Lancers arrived to relieve No 3 and 4 coys of the Batn.	
8.30 pm	Relief completed and been having collected on had been regimental first aid post handed to Subedar at LE HAMEL.	
LE HAMEL – BILLETS		
Nov. 24"		
Nov. 25"		
Nov. 26" 4.30 pm	Received orders to march at once and relieve 6th JATS in billets, and act as reserve to FEROZEPORE BDE.	
	Went into billets in large farm house about 250 x from 6th JATS, on RUE DE BETHUNE	
Nov. 27" 3. pm	Small 15" gunner field gun commenced shelling farm. One shell caught top of house – No 1 and 2 coys located farm to his right 3 and 4 to his left and took shelter in natural ditches alongside road 1 man slightly wounded outside farm.	

Army Form C. 2118.

WAR DIARY

of 1/9 GR

INTELLIGENCE SUMMARY.

(Erase heading not required.)

Instructions regarding War Diaries and Intelligence Summaries are contained in F. S. Regs., Part II, and the Staff Manual respectively. Title pages will be prepared in manuscript.

Hour, Date, Place.	Summary of Events and Information.	Remarks and references to Appendices.
BILLETS. — nr. FESTUBERT.		
Nov. 28"		
" 29		
" 30.	Received orders to remain in readiness — Received orders that we should go into the trenches on night of 2/3" Dec. and be attached to Bareilly Bde.	
DEC. 1"		
" 2." 9. a.m.	C.O, Adjt. and coy. commanders went up to reconnoitre trenches of LEFT SECTION.	
4. p.m.	Right half Batn. marched up to the trenches.	
4.30 p.m.	Left half Batn. left billets for the trenches.	
5.45 p.m.	Relief completed.	
	No 1 coy. No 4 coy. 3 sections E. coy	
	Capt Pike. Capt. Mackinnon.	
	FIRING LINE	
	F coy — C. coy	
	Support.	
	D coy	
	Reserve	
LEFT SECTION. TRENCHES. FESTUBERT.		
DEC. 3rd	No change in situation. German trench untaken originally first trench into CENTRE SECTION trenches to right of PICQUET HOUSE.	

Army Form C. 2118.

WAR DIARY
or
INTELLIGENCE SUMMARY.
(Erase heading not required.)

Instructions regarding War Diaries and Intelligence Summaries are contained in F. S. Regs., Part II, and the Staff Manual respectively. Title pages will be prepared in manuscript.

Hour, Date, Place.	Summary of Events and Information.	Remarks and references to Appendices.
LEFT SECTION TRENCHES. FESTUBERT.		
DEC. 3rd cont.	Cloudy weather, with some rain.	
DEC. 4th 1. am.	Fine night. Heavy howitzing heard on left of centre section. Our scouts being handicapped by bright moonlight. Similarly difficult for head hurriers to do any bring. Started to sap out to his left of picquet house. Cold wind cloudy. Rain during night.	
" 5th	Rain most of day – trenches getting very wet and deep in mud. Our sap advanced 6 yards.	
" 6th 9. am	Our aeroplanes being busy, no course down so far that gunners watching opened a heavy rifle fire. German anti-aircraft guns also shelled aeroplanes heavily.	
2.15 pm.	German saps near picquet house bombarded by our Siege battery. German infantry kept up heavy rifle fire during night. B We brought up materials for head proof shelters. Lt. ASHMORE, 10th GR joined.	

WAR DIARY or INTELLIGENCE SUMMARY.

Army Form C. 2118.

Instructions regarding War Diaries and Intelligence Summaries are contained in F.S. Regs., Part II, and the Staff Manual respectively. Title pages will be prepared in manuscript.

(Erase heading not required.)

Hour, Date, Place.	Summary of Events and Information.	Remarks and references to Appendices.
LEFT SECTION TRENCHES FESTUBERT.		
Dec. 7th 2.30 pm	Rain. Trenches in very bad condition especially communication trenches, over 1 foot deep in places with water.	
8th	Our heavy guns bombarded German trenches during night. All quiet.	
9th	Germans bombed our right trenches with trench mortars — no damage done.	
10th 11th 12th 13th	40 Rifles 8th Hussars posted in our trenches. No change. Our Saps advanced some 20 yards. Trenches getting deep in water on our right. Communication with to FESTUBERT two feet deep in water in places. Rain nearly every day — but held.	
14th	Rain. Ordered to fire slow converging at 10 o'clock and to continue list whole day. Bomb throwers went out at night and threw bombs into Sap No. 2 and German trench near Picquet house. During night we made a traverse in hatured ditch to prevent it was discovered that gunmen had put up traverse in Sap head No 2.	have Sepoy wounded by gunman rifle grenade.
15th	Rain.	

Army Form C. 2118.

WAR DIARY
or
INTELLIGENCE SUMMARY.

(Erase heading not required.)

Instructions regarding War Diaries and Intelligence Summaries are contained in F. S. Regs., Part II, and the Staff Manual respectively. Title pages will be prepared in manuscript.

Hour, Date, Place.	Summary of Events and Information.	Remarks and references to Appendices.
LEFT SECTION TRENCHES. FESTUBERT.		
Dec. 16th Billets rue de Lepinette		
17th }		
18th }		
19th 7. am	Relieved by Seaforths at 9.pm and went into billets in the Rue-de-Lepinette. Issued great coats.	
20th 7. am	Right half battalion under Major Boignell ordered out in reserve to 2-2nd K.E.O Gurkhas. Right half battalion returned to billets.	
about 10. am	Received orders to take whole Baton up to hit 2nd G.R trenches. Started whilst moving up Rue du Bois & whilst crossing open fields knew 6" Jat the Gurkhas as we came into open fields, came under fairly heavy rifle fire, but knew very inaccurate. Major BOILEAU and MAJOR HOLT of 2nd G.R who had been forced to retire to trench at near end of STRAND. Told us that Germans were in STRAND. Capt. hackinnon ordered to take houses on N. side of CHOCOLATE MENIER road — and push up towards Germans as far as possible. Patrol under Lt MURRAY pushed up the Strand. Gurkhas who were in the Strand and trenches moving with it, seeing large reinforcements coming up, retired to main trench in orchard, as Lieut hill fire died down. Lt MURRAY with patrol pushed about 200 yards up the strand and	2 men wounded

WAR DIARY
or
INTELLIGENCE SUMMARY.

Army Form C. 2118.

Hour, Date, Place.	Summary of Events and Information.	Remarks and references to Appendices.
ORCHARD TRENCHES S.E. of Rue du Lépinette DEC. 20th 12. Noon	and built a traverse across it, at his bend little which runs at right angles to CHOCOLATE MENIER road. Colonel WIDDICOMBE went up to right company of 6th JATS trench, about a company of 2nd G.R. were still holding him there. Captain ROSS 6th JATS informed Colonel Widdicombe that the garrison were in strength, and that in his opinion it would require at least two battalions to make a counter attack. At dusk Lt ROGERS with No 3 coy was ordered to push forward as far as possible and dig himself in linking up with 6th Jats left and our No 4 coy which was digging itself in on left side of the bit STRAND. Our guns bombarded his garrison most of the night, our shells falling very close in front of our companies who were digging, and occasionally behind them. A Jaffer officer was sent up to us in conjunction with his coy of 2nd G.R. in right of 6th Jats, was to attempt to turn his garrison out of their trench, he was ordered to occupy his trench when captured, attempt was given up however.	

DEC 21st

Army Form C. 2118.

WAR DIARY or INTELLIGENCE SUMMARY.

(Erase heading not required.)

Instructions regarding War Diaries and Intelligence Summaries are contained in F. S. Regs., Part II, and the Staff Manual respectively. Title pages will be prepared in manuscript.

Hour, Date, Place.	Summary of Events and Information.	Remarks and references to Appendices.
ORCHARD TRENCHES. S.E of LEPINETTE. DEC. 21st		
6. pm.	Put our sharpshooters on to sniping the gunners. Accounted for four of them, and stopped them working loopholes or machine gun emplacement. A counter attack on Gurkhas made by Northamptons and Northamps. 58th Rifles (on our right) and machine gunners cooperating with rifle fire, and machine gun fire. Counted got into touch with his counter attack. Sent a patrol up his Strand, but an officer in the Northamptons who said they had lost heavily, and having lost touch with Northamps on his right had had to return to his Strand after having crossed the COCOA/T MENIER road. Reports that so far as we knew the counter attack had failed. Quiet during rest of night.	
Dec. 22nd		
6.30 am.	2nd G.R. went back, having been relieved.	
7. am.	Heavy harass fire started; but Gurkhas made a counter attack on Northamps who were in trenches on our side of his orchard. Enemy came under our rifle fire as they moved from our left to our right - moving behind orchard	

Army Form C. 2118.

WAR DIARY
or
INTELLIGENCE SUMMARY.

(Erase heading not required.)

Instructions regarding War Diaries and Intelligence Summaries are contained in F. S. Regs., Part II, and the Staff Manual respectively. Title pages will be prepared in manuscript.

Hour, Date, Place.	Summary of Events and Information.	Remarks and references to Appendices.
TRENCHES - RUE DE LEPINETTE		
DEC. 22nd	They evidently seem got round North Lanes, right flank & commenced firing hard grenades at team on their front and right flank. About one hundred of them North Lanes retired and suffered heavily from Maxim fire. North had plans finding their position untenable, retired through and down the strand. Quiet for rest of day and during night. We filled up as much of the communication trenches leaving only our fire trench as possible.	
DEC. 23rd	Own men brought in several wounded Inkatoos men. Quiet during day and night.	
DEC. 24th 11.30 p.m.	"Minenwerfer" started firing from behind Orchard House towards trenches in front of Brewery. Sent urgent message to gunners to shell hs Orchard, on "MINENWERFER" position. Relieved by IRISH GUARDS	
DEC. 25th 9.30 am	Marched to BILLETS at VIEILLE CHAPELLE at LE CROIX MARMEUSE. Visited by General Anderson and received his congratulations for doing well in a difficult situation. Have been very hard hit from past.	
DEC. 26th 8.30 am	Marched to billets at ROBECQ	
DEC. 27th 8 am	" " at BAILLEUL aux PERNES via LILLERS about 12 miles	

Army Form C. 2118.
29

WAR DIARY
or
INTELLIGENCE SUMMARY.
(Erase heading not required.)

Instructions regarding War Diaries and Intelligence Summaries are contained in F. S. Regs., Part II, and the Staff Manual respectively. Title pages will be prepared in manuscript.

Hour, Date, Place.	Summary of Events and Information.	Remarks and references to Appendices.
BILLETS. BALLEUL		
DECEMBER 28th		
" 29th 8.55pm	Col Widdicombe, Captain Keyland, Lt MURRAY proceeded on 7 days leave to England via BOULOGNE	
" 30th		
" 31st		
JANUARY 1st 1915		
" 2nd		
" 3rd	Inspected by General Willcocks	
" 4th		
" 5th		
WED. 6th	Inspected by General French.	
" 7th	Captain Pike, Lt Pryder, Major Bignell, Col Daly I.M.S proceeded on 7 days leave.	
" 8th		
SUNDAY 9th	Mens clothes washed and ironed.	
" 10th		
" 11th	Parades consist not entrenching - trench knowing -	
" 12th	bayonet from the trench.	

121/4401

WAR DIARY
OF
1/9th Gurkhas.

From 13th January 1915 To 29th January 1915.

Army Form C. 2118.

31

WAR DIARY
or
INTELLIGENCE SUMMARY.

1/9 GR

(Erase heading not required.)

Instructions regarding War Diaries and Intelligence Summaries are contained in F. S. Regs., Part II, and the Staff Manual respectively. Title pages will be prepared in manuscript.

Hour, Date, Place.	Summary of Events and Information.	Remarks and references to Appendices.
BILLETS. BAILLEUL aux PERNES.		
JAN. 13th 1915 Wednesday	Capt Mackinnon, Lt Berry, Lt Kent proceeded on leave. Capt Pine, Lt Poynder, Major Bigneli, 2nd Lt Daly rejoined from leave.	
14th		
15th		
16th	Parade carried out chiefly entrenching — recruits drill daily.	
Sunday 17th		
18th	B.O.'s and 2nd G.O.'s went to see exhibition of horse winning and attacking trenches.	2.8 19th Military Police
19th	Major Champain and four Kalladadars and 103 N.C.O.'s and men joined the Batn.	
20th		
21st	Brigade Route march.	
22nd	Parade.	
23rd	General Anderson inspected the recently arrived draft. Battalion marched at 9 a.m. for billets in CAZONNE via LILLERS — Appendix B.	STRENGTH OF BATTN. B.O.'s 11 including M.O. G.O.'s 17 N.C.O.'s Priv: 748.
11 am	BOSNES and ROBECQ. Reached LILLERS.	
12.30 pm	"L'ECLEME" where we entrained in lorries and drove to CAZONNE — Bright cold weather with frost.	
Sunday 24th		
11 am	Marched to Pailette at VIEILLE CHAPELLE (orders Appendix B)	
25th	Detailed to be Brigade in waiting.	
26th		
10.30	Battalion Route march.	
5 pm	Battalion in waiting.	

R Widdicombe
Lt Col Comdg
1/9 GR

Army Form C. 2118.

32

WAR DIARY
or
INTELLIGENCE SUMMARY.
(Erase heading not required.)

Instructions regarding War Diaries and Intelligence Summaries are contained in F. S. Regs., Part II, and the Staff Manual respectively. Title pages will be prepared in manuscript.

Hour, Date, Place.	Summary of Events and Information.	Remarks and references to Appendices.
BILLETS. VIELLE CHAPELLE. JANUARY 27th 1915. (WED)	Very heavy rifle fire from direction of NEUVE CHAPELLE at about 11 p.m.	
	Heavy bombardment by our guns from about 1 a.m.	
16 5.30 a.m.	300 men sent out as working party.	
5 p.m.	100 men sent out as working party.	
9 p.m.	200 men sent out as working party.	
28th 9 a.m.	200 " " " " "	A heavy frost on morning from 24th on 26.1.15
12.30 p.m.	Received orders as to relieving GARHWAL BRIGADE in front line. (Appendix B)	
5 p.m.	200 men sent out as working party at 9 a.m. and 12.30 p.m; and 100 men for carrying.	
29th 1 p.m.	Battalion marched to hts billets occupied by LEICESTER regiment in lst Rue des BERCEAUX.	G. Widdicombe Lt Col Cmdg 1/3 G.R.
2 p.m.	Reached hts Rue des BERCEAUX.	
2.15 p.m.	Relief completed 400 men sent out at 9 p.m. as working party.	

Gulab Singh & Sons, Calcutta—No. 22 Army C.—5-8-14—1,07,000.

War Diary APPENDIX B

Operation Order No 12
by
Brigadier General C. W. Jacob.
Commanding Dehra Dun Brigade

CHATEAU. FERFAY.
20th January 1915.

Ref map 1/80000. — ST OMER and ARRAS.

Information 1. The Brigade plus No 4 Coy Sappers and Miners, will move to CALONNE, en route to VIEILLE CHAPELLE on January 23rd 1915.

Orders to troops 2.(a) The head of the Brigade will pass the starting point the Railway level crossing at LILLERS as under:—
Brigade Head Quarters at 10-30 a.m. route via HURIONVILLE.
1st Seaforths at 10-30 a.m. via FERFAY and HURIONVILLE.
6th Jats at 10-40 a.m. } via RAIMBERT and BURBURE.
2nd Gurkhas at 10-50 a.m. }
9th Gurkhas at 11 a.m. via AUMERVAL, FERFAY and HURIONVILLE
A & B 19 B.F.A. } at 11-10 a.m. via RAIMBERT and BURBURE.
128 J.F.A

(b). Route from LILLERS will be BUSNES and ROBECQ.
(c). Baggage section of Units will march in rear of the Bde under orders of Capt. BROOKE, No 2 Coy Divisional Train and representatives of Units will report to him at the cross roads S E of ST NICHOLAS at 11-15 a.m. Waggons of Bde Head Quarters, 1st Seaforths and 9th Gurkhas will be formed up by that hour on the ST NICHOLAS — FERFAY road in above order, with leading waggon just short of cross roads. Waggons of 6th Jats, 2nd Gurkhas and Field ambulances will follow 128 JFA and will halt at cross roads. On arrival in billets representatives will be sent to the South entrance of CALONNE to lead baggage waggons to billets.
No 4 Coy Sappers and Miners will march independently from MANQUEVILLE to CALONNE

371/W.
21-1-15

via BUSNES. The march should be so timed that ROBECQ is not reached before 11 am or after 12-20 pm.

Billeting Parties. 3. Billeting parties of units to report to Captain WICKS, 1st Seaforths at the South entrance of CALONNE at 11 am.

Supplies. 4. Refilling Point- BORECQ 9 am, 23rd January. Supply waggons will be met at ROBECQ at 1 pm by a Staff Officer and led to the billeting area.

Reports. 5. Reports to the Head of the Column.

Issued at 6-30 pm.

H.N. Salter
Major,
Brigade Major Dehra Dun Bde.

{ Copy No 1 and 2 to War Diary
Copy No 3 to 1st Seaforths
Copy No 4 to 6th Jats
Copy No 5 to 9th Gurkhas
Copy No 6 to 2nd Gurkhas
Copy No 7 to No 4 Coy Sappers & Miners
Copy No 8 to No 2 Coy Meerut Divisional Train
Copy No 9 to Meerut Division
Copy No 10 to 19 B.F.A.
Copy No 11 to 128 J.F.A.

To Brigade Supply Section for distribution

Head Quarters Dehra Dun Brigade
22nd January 1915

The following is substituted for para 3 of Operation Order
No 12, dated 20th January 1915:-

Orders to troops

(a) Seventy lorries will be on the DUNKERQUE Road at 10-45 a.m. facing North East — tail at the ST NICHOLAS cross roads covering a distance of 1400 yards — each lorry will hold 20 men. The 6th Jats will entrain in the leading 24 lorries. The 2nd Gurkhas will entrain in the next 36 lorries. Approximately 200 1st Seaforths will entrain in the last 10 lorries. The lorries will be allotted by the O.C. 6th Jats under whose orders the lorries will run via RAIMBERT — BURBURE — HAUT RIEUX — BAS RAUX — BUSNETTES — to the road junction immediately south of L'ECLEME. The lorries should start as soon after 11 a.m. as possible. When the leading lorry reaches the road junction the above troops will detrain and march to CALONNE via ROBECQ under orders of Lieut Colonel Roche, 6th Jats. The lorries will be sent on to halt on a length 1400 yards on the L'ECLEME — BUSNES road to pick up the remainder 1st Seaforths & 9th Gurkhas. The Bde Major will report to the O.C. 6th Jats at ST NICHOLAS cross roads at 10-20 a.m. to assist in marshalling lorries etc.

(b) The 1st Seaforths (less approximately 200 men) will march at 9 a.m. via FERFAY — HURIONVILLE — LILLERS — CANTRAMNE to L'ECLEME and form up on the BUSNES road ready to entrain at 12 noon. The leading lorry will be halted at a suitable point vide (a) above. The 9th Gurkhas will follow the 1st Seaforths. 34 lorries will be allotted to 1st Seaforths 36 " " " " 9th Gurkhas

The move will be under the order of Lieut Col Widdicombe, 9th Gurkhas. The above will detrain at CALONNE.

(c). Machine guns & transport of the Seaforths and 9th Gurkhas will follow in rear of the 19 B.F.A and move to CALONNE via LILLERS - BUSNES and ROBECQ under orders of senior officer present.

(d). Machine guns & transport of 6th Jats and 2nd Gurkhas will pass ST NICHOLAS cross roads at 9-30 am and move via LILLERS - BUSNES - ROBECQ to CALONNE under orders of senior officer.

(e) The Officer of No 2 Coy Divisional train will be at level crossing LILLERS at 10-30 am to marshal the transport mentioned in (c), (d) and (g).

(f) The 19 B.F.A will march in rear of the 9th Gurkhas. The 12? J.F.A will pass ST NICHOLAS cross roads at 9-15 am and march via LILLERS - BUSNES and ROBECQ to CALONNE. 2 ambulances will await 6th Jats and 9th Gurkhas at ROBECQ.

(g) Bde Head Quarters will march to CALONNE at 9am via LILLERS - BUSNES and ROBECQ

Issued at 11-30 pm.

H. Walker, Major
Bde Major Dehra Dun Bde

Copy No 1 & 2 to War Diary
    "   3   to 1st Seaforths
    "   4   to 6th Jats
    "   5   to 9th Gurkhas
    "   6   to 2nd Gurkhas
    "   7   to O.C. No 2 Coy Div train
    "   8   to 19 BFA
    "   9   to 12? JFA
    "   10   to Meerut Div

Urgent
9th Gurkhas

67

APPENDIX B

Orders No 12
by
Brigadier General A.B. Scott
Commanding Dehra Dun Bde

CALONNE 23rd January 1915

Reference map France (BETHUNE) 1/40,000.

Information
1. (a) The Dehra Dun and Garhwal Bdes are to form a detachment under Brig General A.B. SCOTT. CB, DSO and will take over a section of the front of the 1st Corps.
(b) The Bde is to move to VIEILLE CHAPELLE tomorrow January 24th

Orders to Troops
2. (a) The head of the column, as under, will pass the starting point — the road junction square Q 11 b n at 11 a.m. — Route square Q 11 b — Q 11 d — LE GOUZATEUX FE — L'EPINETTE — square R 7.d — cross roads R 9.c — RUE DEL ANNOY — FOSSE — square R 28.b.
(b). The ROBECQ - CALONNE - LESTREM road is to be kept clear for motor transport till 10-45 a.m. No troops or carts are to be brought on to the road till that hour.
(c). The cyclists of all battalions under the Scout Officers of the Jats and 9th Gurkhas will go ahead of the column leaving men at road junctions to show route and also to side track traffic which would interfere with the march.

Order of march:—
Bde Hd Quarters (less Bde Signal Section) 11 a.m.
1st Seaforths 11 a.m.
Signal Section 11-15 a.m.
Machine Gun Section 107th Pioneers 11-20 a.m.
6th Jats 11-25 a.m.
4 Coy 2/8 M 11-40 a.m.
2nd Gurkhas 11-50 a.m.
9th Gurkhas 12-5 pm
A/18 · 19 BFA } 12-20 pm
128 I FA }

No 409/c
24-1-15

Billetting
3. Billetting parties to report to Capt Wicks, 1st Seaforths at cross roads square R-28 at 12 noon

Transport 4. Transport with units

Reports 5. In head of the column.

Issued at 7.30 pm

T. T. Walker
Major
Brigade Major Dehra Dun Bde

Copies 1 & 2 War Diary
" 3 1st Seaforths
" 4 6th Jats
" 5 9th Gurkhas
" 6 2nd Gurkhas
" 7 Meerut Division
" 8. 2 Coy Div train
" 9 19 B F A
" 10 13 ? F A
" 11. M G detachment - 107 pioneers
" 12. 4 Coy Sappers & Miners.

9th Gurkhas Urgent

Operation Order No. 14
by
Brigadier General C.W. Jacob.
Commanding Dehra Dun Brigade

Copy No. 5
APPENDIX B

LA COUTURE
28th January 1915.

Information 1. (a) The Dehra Dun Brigade to relieve the Garhwal Brigade tomorrow January 29th.
(b) During the relief the Dehra Dun Brigade will use the road South of LA LOUANNE river and Garhwal Brigade the road North of the river.

Orders to Troops. 2 (a). The 9th Gurkhas and 2nd Gurkhas will relieve the Leicesters and 1/39th Garhwalis in RUE DES BERCEAUX and RICHEBOURG ST VAAST respectively. The battalions will time their marches to arrive at 2 pm. The relieved battalions will be drawn up outside their billets and march off on relief.

(b). The 6th Jats and 1st Seaforths will march so as to arrive at the Head Quarters of Sub Sections C1 and C2 respectively at 5-30 pm when they relieve the 2/39th Garhwal Rifles and 2/3rd Gurkhas in the front line.

(c) The garrisons of Redoubts need not be found tomorrow night 29th/30th. In case of necessity the garrisons will be found by the battalions in C1 and C2 respectively from their reserve Companies. On other nights they will be furnished by the 2nd Gurkhas or 6th Jats whichever is not holding the front line.

Machine Guns 3. (a). Machine Guns of 107th Pioneers and 6th Jats will be attached to Subsection C1.

(b). Machine Guns of 2nd Gurkhas, 4th Cavalry, 1st Seaforths and 1/9th Gurkhas will be attached to Subsection C2.

(c) Guns of 4th Cavalry and 107th Pioneers will remain in position.

(d). Guns of 2/2nd Gurkhas and 1/9th Gurkhas will report to the O.C. 1st Seaforths at LA COUTURE at 4 pm and will relieve two gun sections of the Garhwal Brigade. The gun section of the 2/2nd Gurkhas should have the position nearest the right of C2 so as to enable them to be near their own battalion when it comes

No 480/W
29.1.15

comes up into the front line and the Subsections are readjusted.

Transport 4. (a) No transport is to reach RICHEBOURG ST VAAST before 1-15 pm.

(b) Battalions in front line will return baggage and baggage wagons to No 2 Coy Divisional Train at FOSSE.

(c) The other two battalions may have their baggage if required but empty carts are to be returned to No 2 Coy Divisional Train at FOSSE.

(d) First line transport will be billeted as under:—
1st Seaforths — billets of 1st line transport of Leicesters
Bde Head Quarters & 6th Jats — Farm Court ST VAAST square X·5-b.
9th Gurkhas — Farm in square R-36 a.c.
2nd Gurkhas — Farm in square R-35 (centre)

5. Some of these are at present occupied by Garhwal Bde.
Ammunition transport but will be vacated.

5. Garhwal Bde battalions in front line will hand over roughly 200 rounds SAA per rifle; also some bombs and very pistol cartridges.

Reports: 6. The General Officer Commanding Garhwal Brigade will remain in command of the line until the reliefs are completed. The Head Quarters Dehra Dun Brigade will be established in same house.

Issued at 4-35 pm.   A.Walker.
                              Major
                    Brigade Major Dehra Dun Bde.

Copy 1 & 2 War Diary   Copy 11. Garhwal Bde
 "   3. 1st Seaforths   "   12. No Bde R.F.A.
 "   4. 6th Jats
 "   5. 9th Gurkhas
 "   6. 2nd Gurkhas
 "   7. 3 Coy S & M
 "   8. Meerut Detachment.
 "   9. 128 J F A
 " 10. 19 B F A

Issue these orders

1. The Dehra Dun Bde will relieve the Garhwal Bde tomorrow Jan 29th.
2. The Battn will relieve the Leicesters billeted in Rue du Bercaux, at 2 pm tomorrow; marching there via the road S. of LA LOUANNE
3. The M/G Sec of the Battn under Lt Berry will report to OC 1st Seaforths at LA COUTURE at 4 pm.
4. No transport is to reach Richebourg St Vaast before 1.15 pm.
5. First line transport only will accompany the Battn & will be billeted in farm — Sq. R.36.A.C. 2nd Line Trans to No 2 Coy Divl
6. D.D. Bde H.Q. will be in time Louee at FOSSE Garhwal Bde H.Q. Sq.
7. G.O.C. Garhwal Bde will remain in command until reliefs are completed.
8. Whole of above Battn will parade at

Serial No 96.

121/4719

WAR DIARY.
with Appendix B.

1/9th Gurkha Rifles.

From 30th January 1915 To 26th February 1915.

Army Form C.2118.
33

WAR DIARY
or
INTELLIGENCE SUMMARY.
(Erase heading not required.)

Instructions regarding War Diaries and Intelligence Summaries are contained in F. S. Regs., Part II, and the Staff Manual respectively. Title pages will be prepared in manuscript.

Hour, Date, Place.	Summary of Events and Information.	Remarks and references to Appendices.
BILLETS — RUE du BERCEAUX. JAN. 30. 1915 8.30 pm. 31.	Working parties sent out to work behind front line. MAJOR BIGNELL and LT. KEMP with working party of 250 men went out at 8.30 pm. Received orders to relieve 1st SEAFORTHS in front line (AP. B)	
FEB. 1st 5: pm.	Battalion paraded for relief of SEAFORTHS in the following order. Nos 2 - 1 Coys. here to picquets leading each coy. here to picquets were well smeared with whale oil prior to marching off.	
5.15 pm	Met by guides from 1st SEAFORTHS.	
8.15 pm	Relief complete. SECTION of line taken over by Battalion C 2, C 1 being taken over by 2w Gorkhas on our right. C 2 extended from facing chimney inclusive to LABASSÉE — ESTAIRES road exclusive.	
Feb. 2. 5.15 am	Here from wet picquets reports on being relieved and were sent back to his drying station near his Rue du Berceaux. Major Colonel Macfarlane of his 4th Seaforths and his Brigade Major came up to see his line.	

Army Form C. 2118.

34

WAR DIARY
or
INTELLIGENCE SUMMARY.

(Erase heading not required.)

Hour, Date, Place.	Summary of Events and Information.	Remarks and references to Appendices.
TRENCHES. RICHEBOURG ST VAAST.		
Feb. 2nd (continued) 6.30 p.m.	The 4th Seaforths are to take up our Right Subsection and our left is to be prolonged to the Rue du Bois. One coy. 4th Seaforths relieved Captain PIKE and No 1. coy. who went back into RESERVE in place of No 4 coy. No 4 coy. sent up 100 men to occupy new trench on our left. Rain during day - ground very heavy. Orders for above were as Appendix B.	
Feb. 3rd.	Fine morning. Leicesters C.O. and 1/39 Garhwalis came to Battn HdQrs. to look over lines. Received relief orders (see Appendix. B). Issued orders to relieve (App B).	
Feb. 4th.	Relieving regiments came up at 5.45 p.m.	
9.35 p.m.	Relief completed. Coys on relief marched back independently to billets in VIELLE CHAPELLE.	

Army Form C. 2118.

35

WAR DIARY
or
INTELLIGENCE SUMMARY.

(Erase heading not required.)

Instructions regarding War Diaries and Intelligence Summaries are contained in F. S. Regs., Part II, and the Staff Manual respectively. Title pages will be prepared in manuscript.

Hour, Date, Place.	Summary of Events and Information.	Remarks and references to Appendices.
BILLETS. VIELLE CHAPELLE.		
FEB. 5th	Parades – close order drill.	
6th	Captain PIKE and 150 men from No 1. Coy. marched out as working party to Hd Qrs. LEICESTER regiment. Parades. Close order drill – rifle exercises – firing exercises.	
5.pm	BATTALION in waiting. Heavy firing from our guns. Heard that the attack on CUINCHY had been successful.	
FEB 7th Sunday.	Parades as for the 6th Feb.	
" 8th Mon 11.30 am	Received orders to march to hutts at QUENTIN and PACAUT. Marched to QUENTIN.	
" 9th	Parades under company commanders. Rain.	
" 10th 10. am	Coy. kit inspections. FINE frosty day.	
3.pm	" parades.	
" 11th 10. am	Coy Route marching.	
3.pm	" Parades.	
" 12th 10 am	" Parades. Major Champain granted 7 days leave to England	
3.pm	" Parades. Lt Howroyd rejoined from H.Q. Army	
" 13th	Heavy rain.	

Army Form C. 2118.

36

WAR DIARY
or
INTELLIGENCE SUMMARY.
(Erase heading not required.)

Hour, Date, Place.	Summary of Events and Information.	Remarks and references to Appendices.
BILLETS. QUENTIN.		
Sunday. FEBRUARY. 14th	Heavy Rain.	
15th	Route march.	
3.pm	Company paraded. ⎫	
16th	⎬ Fine weather.	
10.am	" paraded.	
3.pm	" paraded. ⎭	
17th	Heavy Rain.	
18th	Route march. Major Champain rejoined from 7 days leave.	
19th		
10.am	Coy paraded.	
3.pm	" paraded.	
20th	Route march.	
4.pm	Bomb throwing practice.	
Sunday. 21st	Received orders to march to VIEILLE CHAPELLE on his 22nd and to take over a section of his front line on 23rd Feb.	APPENDIX. B.
22nd	Marched to huts in VIEILLE CHAPELLE.	
23rd 1.pm	Marched to RICHEBOURG ST VAAST and took over trenches	
5.30pm	Occupied by 57th RIFLES. Working party of 100 men detailed.	

Army Form C. 2118.

37

WAR DIARY
or
INTELLIGENCE SUMMARY.

(Erase heading not required.)

Hour, Date, Place.	Summary of Events and Information.	Remarks and references to Appendices.
BILLETS. RICHEBOURG ST. VAAST. FEB.	In rovert to DEHRA DUN BRIGADE.	
WEDNESDAY 24th 6.30 p.m.	Two British Officers and 250 men detailed as working party in Rue du Bois.	
7.30 p.m.	One hundred men detailed as carrying party.	One man killed.
10.30 p.m.	Received message from Brigade that enemy showed unusual activity in some of their trenches, and ordered to be ready to turn out at very short notice. Show.	APPENDIX B.
Feb. 25th 7. p.m.	Carrying party of 100 men detailed. Fine.	
Feb. 26th 6.30 p.m.	Carrying party of 100 men.	
7.0 p.m.	" " " "	
7.30 p.m.	1 Punjabi Officer and 150 men of No 3. company detailed for work in the Rue du Bois. Fine day.	

G. Wigtocombe
Lt. Col.
Cmdg. 1/9 G.R.

~~Operation Orders.~~

No. ~~by~~   war diary

Daily Report   Place
No 3 Company   Date 2.2.15

The Company took over the left Section of the trenches at 5-30 p.m. 1st February. Piquets and Sentries were posted in the places occupied by the relieved regiment.

The Piquets in the "wet" trenches report that their actual piquet posts are fairly dry, but muddy, while the trenches on either side as well as the communication trench are nearly waist-deep in water. They did not move up or down the Communication trenches and consequently had not got wet. I therefore did not send them back to the drying station.

Desultory rifle firing continued throughout the night and for a great part of the time the enemy could be heard singing in their trenches.

The Enemy sent up flares from time to time but made no attempt to leave their trenches.

How ~~communicated~~
Time.

Operation Orders.

No. **by**

Place

Date

A. J. Combridge & Co., Bombay.

Heavy gun and rifle firing was reported to have been heard about 1 a.m. in the direction of Givenchy and to have lasted for a considerable time.

Since daybreak the rifle firing in our front has slackened considerably.

There have been no casualties in the Company.

As it was the first night in the position the Company remained in the defence trenches till daybreak — but for tonight I have arranged to carry on some work leaving only sentries in the trenches.

H B Champain Major
Comm'g No 3 Co'y

How communicated

Time. 10.30 a.m.

The Adjutant
1/9 Gurkha Rifles.

To adjutant 1/4th L.R.   2.2.15

1) Relief of Centre Section C 2 was carried
   out successfully.
2) Wet picket was relieved at 5 a.m. &
   sent to Battn. Hd. Qrs. to dry.
3) 1 S.O., 1 N.C.O, & 10 men arrived from No. 4 Coy
   to make up numbers.
4) Reports received.
   (a) The enemy singing most of the night
   (b) occasional flares
   (c) very little shooting done by enemy.
   (d) Heavy firing GIVENCHY direction
       about 1 a.m.
5) Patrols to No 1 Coy., & between platoons
   & pickets (incl.ps wet picket) all through
   the night.
6) No work done by Centre Section, several
   working parties from other units are
   at work

                              B. H. Bignell
                                  Major
10.25 am   O.C. No 2 Coy   56

Operation Orders.

No. by

No 3 Company ~~Daily Report~~

Place

Date 3. 11. 15.

1. In accordance with orders received No 3 Company withdrew towards the East yesterday Evening and occupied the new position in the Orchard - handing over No 7 Piquet and the Observation Post to No 4 Company -

The New positions occupied by No 3 Coy are shewn on the accompanying rough sketch -

2. The Enemy fired (rifle) more heavily last night about midnight & again at 5 am. but nothing of importance occurred

3. Small working parties were Employed during the night improving defences.

4. No casualties to report

5. Situation unchanged

How communicated

Time.

H B Champain Major
Com No 3 Coy

Adjutant 1/9 GN

3.2.15

To Adjutant 1/9th L.R.

1) No change in the situation
2) As per O.C.'s orders a new line for No 2 Coy was taken up last night.
3) Well picket successfully relieved at 6 p.m. yesterday & 5 a.m. today.
4) Report received that about 150 yards in front of my well picket (No. 4), close to a bare tree, is a German machine gun — this position is being pointed out to the R.A. ranging officer.
5) A trench to join up No 4 picket with the orchards was begun, but only moved a few yards owing to a fairly heavy fire from the enemy, also the use of their searchlights & flares.
6) No casualties.

B.H. Bynell
Major
O.C. No 2 Coy.

To O.C. 9th Gurkhas

No change in the situation.
 Outlying Picquets report enemy quiet during night. Casualties two men wounded moving up to relief.
 Work carried out last night — Barricade thrown across track leading to enemy's lines from Hd Quarters of this Section. Am now improving loopholes, setting houses into a further state of defence, and completing through lateral communication in all blocks of houses.
 Propose traversing the Barrier and improving the outer line of defence tonight.

D Mackenzie Capt
Comdg No 3 double Coy
4th Sea. Hrs.

10.5 am.
3/2/15

To O C
9th Gurkha Rifles

Operation Orders.

No.   by   War diary

Daily Report   Place
No 3 Company
1/9 Gurkhas   Date 4.2.15

A. J. Combridge & Co., Bombay.

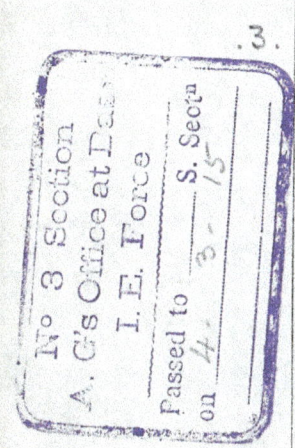

1. Nothing unusual has occurred during the past 24 hours and the situation remains unchanged.

2. During the night I improved the front parapet of the orchard redoubt and have made a good kneeling position all along with bullet proof parapet.

3. At 6.15 pm I received a message from the O.C. Company 4 Seaforth Highlanders on our right, to the effect that a sniper had been firing into one of their piquets from a tree near our right section during the afternoon. He did not definitely [see?] tree but at 8 pm he sent an officer to me who pointed out the tree. I sent out scouts to see and have had all the ground and houses in the vicinity searched but without result.

4. I have been unable to connect up by telephone with the E. Lancashire Regiment on our left. As I could not get connection last night I sent

How communicated   out two signallers after dark
Time.   along the line to try and detect any

Operation Orders.

No. by

Place

Date

A. J. Combridge & Co., Bombay.

break in the line. After going some distance they lost the end of the wire which had been cut and, while searching for it, one of the men was wounded by a rifle bullet. As I had no spare wire with me I could not lay a fresh line. My patrol, however, connected up with the E. Lancashire patrol during the night and reported that as I had no wires I could not join up with them and asked them to try and send out a line from their regiment. So far nothing has been done. I would suggest that O.C. Leicester Regiment be informed of this and be advised to bring out sufficient wire to connect up.

5. I regret to report the following casualty in my Co:
N°2587 Dalbahadur Mal. E Co. wounded in orchard.

6. Water level in trenches remains unchanged.

How communicated

Time. 10. a.m.

H B Champain Major
Comdg 3 Co, 1/9 GR

Adjutant
1/9 Gurkha Rifles.

To O.C. 9th Gurkhas   War diary

The general situation is unchanged.
There were two strong outbursts of Rifle fire
during the night; one between 11 & 12 pm and
the other at 4 am. The Picquets report that
the water in the trenches is gradually getting
less, but there are still from two to three
feet of water & mud in Fire trench of No 3
Piquet (Wet Picquet).

I sent out some Sandbags last night in
order to have the fire Trenches improved
where necessary.

The work of loopholing the houses here is
being carried on. I also propose to improve
the bridges across the staked paths today.

D. Mackenzie Capt
Comdg No 3 Double Coy
4th Sec. Hrs.

10 AM
4/7/15

To O/C
9th Gourkhas

The Adjutant 1/5th S.R.

Daily Report 4.2.15

1. Situation unchanged
2. Work done during last night.
   (a) Parapet of fire trench by old observation post improved
   (b) Sandbag wall by the low barricade on the Rue des Bois heightened by two layers of sandbags and parapet extending from it also heightened.

   I pointed this out to the relieving officer of the Leicesters as very position of the line.

   With regard to the screen to be put up I was unable to carry this out as there was no material available.

support branches of willows to be obtained from the R.E.

(c) Portion of barricade at the last house on the right on the Rue du Bois rebuilt

Requirements

Entanglements opposite new new fire trench in front of old observation house, also between trench and Rue du Bois on one side and to the present Gunner observation house on the other side.

The traverses along the new communication trench running parallel to the Rue du Bois from the last house on the right should be heightened as this trench is enfiladed.

(2) Major Champain is reporting about our telephonic communication with the C. Lansdowne.

3. I am handing over to my relief
   26 Picks
   30 Shovels
   23 boxes of ammunition
   and also about four sandbags full of ammunition, that has been left by some regiment.
   Also about 400 empty sandbags.

4. By day and night

I keep 50 men in the fire trench, as I do not consider two groups of six men sufficient.

The remainder (less two piquets) line the Black Adder redoubt.

5. I had one casualty No 2331? Dalbir Adhikari, badly wounded while assisting to mend telephone wire to E Lancashires.

A. Mackenzie Capt
O.C. No IV Coy
4.2.15

To Adjutant
    1/4th S.R.

4.2.15

Report to 9.45 a.m.

1) No change in situation
2) Wet picket relieved at 6 p.m. & 5 a.m.
3) Sausage picket   "   "   6 p.m.
4) Heavy firing reported (& heard) ——
   beyond our right flank at 5.45 a.m.
5) No change in water level
6) Party of 107th Pioneers completed a portion
   of trench in my section - not completed
   yet.
7) No 2730 Rm. Parker Bassett wounded.

B H B Snell
       Major
   O.C. No 2 Coy

A. Dufour
1/2 Geek la Rifle

General Report on right sub-section
C2

1. The trench known as the barrier was joined up last night to the Cinder Track & can now be occupied for firing kneeling when required. The remaining line of resistance has been improved during the night.

2. Communications for each platoon to get rapidly up to its portion of line of resistance have been made; at least 2, & in some 3, communication ways have been made per platoon.

3. The left of the right sub-section is a very bad fire trench & failing other orders I am starting a trench to-night in orchard in front of this.

No.	Date	Time	Place
To:			Place

the present trench here / has no field of fire.

4. Barricades are being made this evening at 2 or 3 points where men have to cross the road & where they are invariably wounded or killed. 1 man killed & 1 wounded in the manner last night. It is understood that previous regiments have lost a certain number of men in going out to the line of resistance. By erecting barricades it is hoped they will catch bullets & screen men going out to the line.

5. Water in trenches does not seem to have subsided. In digging last night water was reached at

From 1 foot level

6. No work seems to have been done on the German sap in front of No 3 piquet.

7. Trenches opposite appear strongly held all along. A fair amount of churning chhurin heard further to the far use on our right (Givenchy - Cuinchy?)

G. D. Fyfe Capt
9th FR
O.C. right sub-section
Cn

Report   10 am

1. Situation unchanged.

2. Work done: during night the parapet of the new fire trench occupied by 50 men of my coy. was improved and two posts made for piquets in the trench. A working party extended the communicating trench to the fire trench joining the same at the old piquet house

3. I am unable to report on the depth of the water, as I have no piquets in wet trenches.

4. Patrols towards the brigade on our left did not join up with their patrols half way. I hear we are in

telephone communication with
them so will get in touch.

5. By day — I have left two
picquets of 1 N.C.O & 3 men
in the new fire trench.
I can reinforce them by
the communicating trench
quickly in case of need.
I withdrew all but the
2 picquets (50 less 8) after
dawn.

6. No casualties

Allenchminralph
O.C. No IV Coy

WAR DIARY or INTELLIGENCE SUMMARY

Army Form C. 2118.

APPENDIX B.

(Erase heading not required.)

Hour, Date, Place.	Summary of Events and Information.	Remarks and references to Appendices.
TRENCHES. RICHEBOURG ST. VAAST. Feb 1st — Feb 4th 9.35 pm	Extent of front was from Chummey enclosure - along Rue du Bois – LA BASSÉE – ESTAIRES ROAD since 1200. Designated C² and divided into Right CENTRE and LEFT SUBSECTIONS - taken over by No 1. coy (Capt Pike) No 2 coy (Major Potquet) and No 3 coy (Major Champain) respectively. Reports had to be submitted to Bde Hd Qrs at 4 am & 4 pm / short reports on general situation 11 am full report. A gap existed between our left and his battalion on our left of some 400x. It was decided to fill this up, and in consequence a trench was dug from his ORCHARD to his Rue du Bois - being to be continued to his left. Casualties during 3 days - 2 killed - 8 wounded and in working parties. 1 killed - 4 [wounded]	map attached Reports attached

G. Widdows [?]
2.o[?]m[?]
Comdg. 1/9 GR |

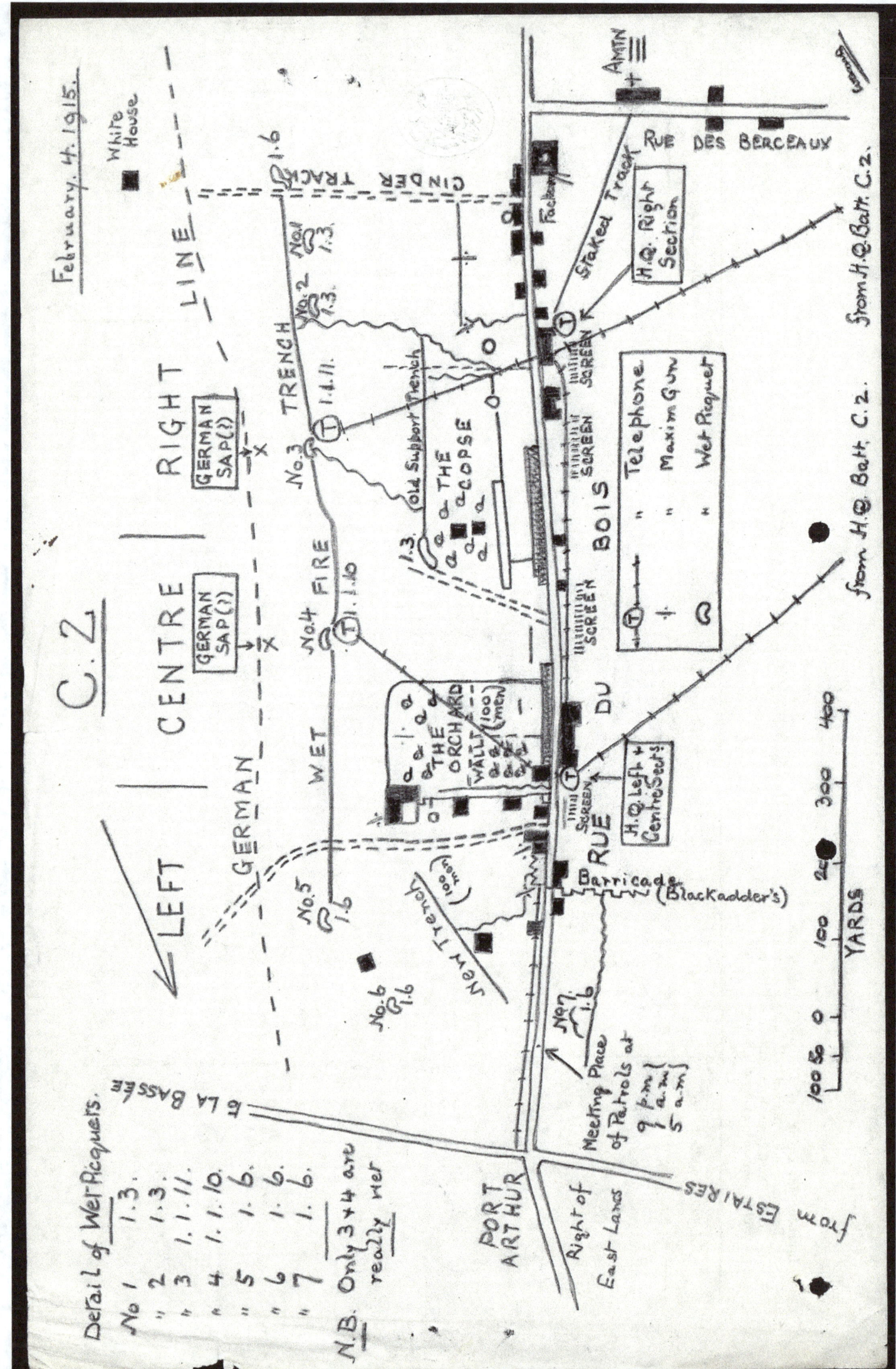

Army Form C. 2118.

APPENDIX. B.

WAR DIARY
or
INTELLIGENCE SUMMARY.

(Erase heading not required.)

Instructions regarding War Diaries and Intelligence Summaries are contained in F. S. Regs., Part II, and the Staff Manual respectively. Title pages will be prepared in manuscript.

Hour, Date, Place.	Summary of Events and Information.	Remarks and references to Appendices.
TRENCHES. RICHEBOURG ST VAAST. FEB 1st — FEB. 4th 9.35pm.	Extent of front was from chimney midway - along Rue du Bois — LA BASSÉE — ESTAIRES Road. Some 1200x. Designated. C. and divided into Right — CENTRE — LEFT SUB-SECTIONS - taken over by No1. coy (Capt PIKE) No 2 coy (Major BIGNELL) and No 3 coys (Major Champain) respectively. Reports had to be submitted to the Brigade at 4. a.m. 4. p.m.} Short report on general situation. 11. a.m — full report. A gap existed between our left and the battalion on our left of some 400x. It was decided to fill this up and in consequence a trench was dug from the orchard to the Rue du Bois — this is to be continued to his left. Casualties during 3 days. 2 killed - 8 wounded. and in the working parties — 1 killed - 4 wounded.	MAP attached. Reports attached

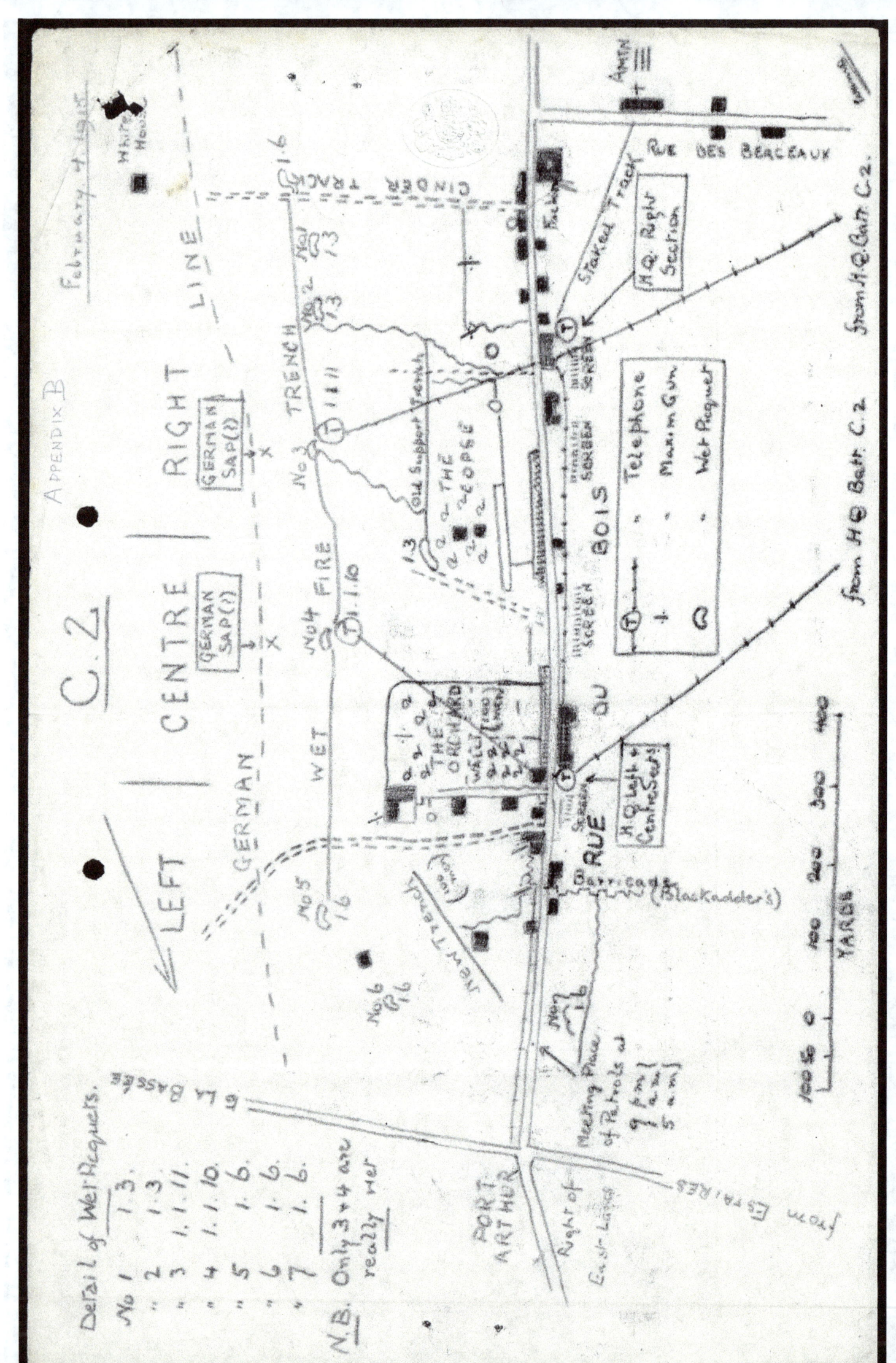

Operation Order No 15
by
Brigadier General C.W. Jacob
Commanding Dehra Dun Brigade

War diary
Appendix B

RICHEBOURG ST VAAST
31st January 1915

Information
1.(a) The 4th Seaforths and ½ 107th Pioneers will join the Brigade tomorrow.
(b) The 6th Jats are under orders to join Bareilly Brigade.

Orders to Troops.
2.(a) The 2nd Gurkhas and 9th Gurkhas will relieve the 6th Jats and Seaforths in Subsections C1 and C2 respectively during the course of tomorrow evening February 1st under arrangements to be made by Officers Commanding Battalions.

(b) On relief the 1st Seaforths will move into the billets vacated by the 9th Gurkhas and will also furnish the garrison of the Redoubt now found by latter battalion.

(c) By 9-30 am tomorrow morning the OC 2nd Gurkhas will have vacated as many billets as possible - closing up as far as possible to the East end of his present billeting area.

(d) The 4th Seaforths will billet temporarily from the defended post S.1.6. to where the 2nd Gurkhas commence. Billeting Officer to report to Bde Head Quarters by 10 am February 1st.

(e) The 4th Seaforths will relieve the garrison (50 rifles) of the Redoubt now held by the 2nd Gurkhas during the course of the day. The relief will be carried out under arrangements to be made by the Officers Commanding the two battalions.

(f) The ½ 107th Pioneers and transport will billet in houses along road N.E. of RICHEBOURG ST VAAST squares S.2.a and M.32.c and d.

(g) On relief the 6th Jats will move into the remaining billets of the 2nd Gurkhas, pending orders for the battalion to join Bareilly Brigade.

W.C. Liuris/ca
d/ 1.2.15

Transport 3. Transport of 4th Seaforths will not follow the battalion to RICHEBOURG ST VAAST but will be met at the cross roads LA COUTURE by the Staff Captain and led to billets. Transport of other Units will remain in present billets.

Issued at 4 pm

J H Walker
Major
Brigade Major Dehra Dun Brigade.

Copy No 1 and 2 retained
Copy No 3   1st Seaforths
Copy No 4   4th Seaforths
Copy No 5   6th Jats
Copy No 6   9th Gurkhas
Copy No 7   2nd Gurkhas
Copy No 8   107th Pioneers
Copy No 9   Meerut Detachment

9th Gurkhas

War diary

Appendix B.

Operation Orders by Lt. Col. G.T. Middicombe
Commanding 9th Gorkhas.

Reference Map
BETHUNE 1/40,000

C². Section.

Feb. 2nd 1915.

1. One Company 4th Seaforths are taking over our right subsection at 7. pm tonight, relieving No 1. Coy which on completion of relief will remain in reserve in billets, now occupied by No 4 Coy.

2. Consequent on the above relief, the following alterations will take place:—

(a) No 2 Coy will relieve the picquet now held by No 1 East of the COPSE.

(b) No 2 Coy will continue to provide No 4 Picquet.

(c) No 3 Coy will relieve the 3 Picquets in the house adjoining to and in the orchard itself (now supplied by No 2 coy).

(d) No 3 Coy will continue to provide picquets Nos. 5 & 6 and in addition will detail a garrison of 100 rifles for the defence of the "ORCHARD".

(e) No 2 Coy's extent of line of defence will remain as it stands at present.

(f) No 3 Coy will be responsible for the defence of the "ORCHARD" and its buildings, which it will hold at all costs.

(G) Two platoons (100 men) of No 4 Coy will move up at 6. pm tonight, and prolong the line of defence from our machine gun House towards "PORT ARTHUR" - keeping one platoon in the new trench which has been constructed East of our left observation post, and one platoon in reserve in billets in the Rue du Bois.

P.T.O

3. O.C. No 1 company will please arrange to have guides at Baton Hd Qrs at 6.15 pm tonight.

J R Heyland
Capt
Adjt 1/9 GR

Circulated for information.
li Officers.
at 3.45 pm

Please initial.

BHB

GSB 3.50
HRL 4.5 pm
MJK
CB 4.20 pm

Officers
9th GR

"A" Form.
Army Form C. 2121

MESSAGES AND SIGNALS.

TO	D	D	BDE

Sender's Number	Day of Month	In reply to Number	
4 R	2/2/15		AAA

PROGRESS	REPORT	UP	TO	NOON.
	C 2	SECTION		
RIGHT	SUB-SECTION			
THE	TRENCH	KNOWN	AS	THE
BARRIER	WAS	JOINED	UP	WHERE
LEFT	UNCOMPLETED	BY	SEAFORTHS	—
TO	THE	CINDER	TRACK	LAST
NIGHT	AND	CAN	NOW	BE
OCCUPIED	FOR	FIRING	KNEELING	aaa
IMPROVEMENTS	CONTINUED	ALONG	REMAINING	LINE
OF	RESISTANCE	aaa		
COMMUNICATIONS	FOR	EACH	PLATOON	TO
RAPIDLY	REACH	ITS	PORTION	OF
LINE	OF	RESISTANCE	HAVE	BEEN
MADE	aaa	TWO	AND	IN
SOME	CASES	THREE	COMMUNICATION	WAY
PER	PLATOON	HAVE	BEEN	MADE

From
Place
Time

MESSAGES AND SIGNALS.

"A" Form. Army Form C.2?

TO: SHEET 2

AAA

THE LEFT OF THE RIGHT SUB SECTION IS A BAD FIRE TRENCH aaa PROPOSE FAILING OTHER ORDERS STARTING A TRENCH TONIGHT IN ORCHARD IN FRONT OF EXISTING TRENCH aaa NO WORK APPEARS TO HAVE BEEN DONE IN FRONT OF NUMBER 3 PICQUET aaa TRENCHES OPPOSITE THIS SUB SECTION APPEAR STRONGLY HELD ALL ALONG aaa CHEERING BY THE GERMANS GREETED THE HEAVY GUN FIRE ON OUR RIGHT AT ABOUT 8.pm IN DIRECTION OF GIVENCHY CENTRE AND LEFT SUBSECTIONS STRENGTHENING DEFENCES OF ORCHARD

"A" Form.　　Army Form C. 2121.
MESSAGES AND SIGNALS.

Sheet 3

and	CONSTRUCTION	OF	FIRING	TRENCH
LEADING	FROM	OUR	LEFT	TO
PORT	ARTHUR	CARRIED	OUT	BY
FATIGUE	PARTIES	UNDER	SUPERVISION	OF
SAPPER	OFFICERS	aaa		

A. Widdicombe - Lt Col.

From Comdg _____ _____

Time 11. am

"A" Form. — War diary — Army Form C. 2121.

MESSAGES AND SIGNALS.

TO	D	D	BDE	

Sender's Number	Day of Month	In reply to Number		AAA
8.R	3			

PROGRESS	REPORT.	C2		
RIGHT	~~SUBSECTION~~	GENERAL		
A	Company	of	fourth	Seaforths
look	over	Right	subsection	from
us	last	night,	and	line
Company	relieved	(our No 1)	was	withdrawn
to	Reserve	and	two	platoons
of	our	company	previously	in
reserve	has	moved	up	to
hold	the	trenches	recently	constructed
prolonging	our	line	towards	Port
Arthur.	Our	No 3 Coy	holds	the
ORCHARD	with	100 rifles	(sketch attached).	
Our	No 2 Coy	forms	up	line
of	defence	between	ORCHARD	and
coy	of	Seaforths	holding	the
Right	Subsection.	We	have	now

From

Place

Time

The above may be forwarded as now corrected. (Z)

"A" Form.
MESSAGES AND SIGNALS.
Army Form C. 2121.

Sheet No 2

one and a half companies in Reserve.

Right Subsection. (1 Coy 4th Seaforths).
No change in situation. Outlying picquets report enemy quiet during night. Work carried out during night - barricade known across track leading towards enemy's lines towards from Hd Qrs of sub section. Loopholes are being improved and though lateral communications between houses being completed.

CENTRE SUBSECTION (No 2 Coy 9th G.R)
No change in situation — a german machine gun was located about 150x in front of west picquet No 4. Position of gun has been pointed out to R.A observing Officer. A communication trench joining up orchard with No 4 picquet was

"A" Form.   Army Form C. 2121.
MESSAGES AND SIGNALS.

LEFT SUBSECTION

Begins. A garrison of 100 rifles posted in orchard and men allotted between posts. Enemies rifle fire last night was heavier about midnight and again at 5 am but nothing of importance occurred. Small working parties employed during the night. No change in situation. Parapet of new trench improved and two posts for piquets made in the communicating trench leading to small house (with dead germans in it) completed.

T. Widdicombe

From: Comdg
Time: 11 am

Operation Order No 16
by
Brigadier General E.W. Jacobs.
Commanding Dehra Dun Brigade.

Appendix B. war diary

RICHEBOURG ST VAAST.
3rd February 1915.

Reference Map France (BETHUNE) 1/40000.

Information.
1. (a) The Garhwal Brigade is to relieve the Dehra Dun Bde in the front line tomorrow, February the 4th.

(b) Troops and Transport going East will use the road South of LA LOUANNE River; those moving West will use the road North of the River.

Orders for Troops.
2. (a) Two half battalions of the Garhwal Bde will arrive at 2-30 pm in RUE DES BERCEAUX and one battalion at 2-30 pm in RICHEBOURG ST VAAST. The 1st Seaforths and 4th Seaforths (less Coy in Front Line) will be clear of their billets by that hour and march to LA COUTURE and VIEILLE CHAPELLE as soon as the relieving Units arrive. The Garrisons of Redoubts A and B near Head Quarters C1 and C2 will remain till relieved by the Garhwal Bde when they will rejoin their battalions. SAA Reserve in Redoubts to be handed over.

(b) The 9th Gurkhas, 2nd Gurkhas and Coy 4th Seaforths in the front line will be relieved under battalion arrangements. Relieving Units of the Garhwal Brigade will arrive at Head Quarters C1 and C2 about 5-45 pm. The Officer Commanding C2 will arrange with the relieving Unit about relief of the Coy 4th Seaforths.

(c) Machine Guns of Dehra Dun Bde will be relieved by guns of Garhwal Bde under arrangements to be made by Officers Commanding C1 and C2 with relieving Units.

(d) Detachments of 4th Cavalry and 107th Pioneers will be relieved by detachments from the Garhwal Bde to whom the guns will be handed over. On relief the detachment 4th Cavalry will march and billet with the 9th Gurkhas. Horses and Transport

7. On relief, Coy Comdrs will march their Coys to Vieille C independently, & by route given in paras above.

The 2 platoons No 4 Coy. & still in reserve on completion of relief, will be under comd of Capt. Pike.

8. Coy Comdrs will report at Bn. H.Q. on completion of their relief.

9. All bombs, rifle grenades, "very" pistol ammunition (not pistols themselves) & gum boots will be handed over to relieving units. Receipts shd. be taken for no. of pairs of Gum boots handed over by Coy Commdrs. Braziers taken in by Coys will be brought [illegible].

10. M/c guns on relief will be man handled to corner on Rue de Berceaux (S.8.B) - where they will meet their mules.

will be sent to 9th Gurkha Head Quarters on the morning of the 5th when detachment will rejoin its Unit. The detachment 107th Pioneers on relief will join the half battalion of its Regiment in RICHEBOURG ST VAAST.

Ammunition *X (c) 3. Units in front line will hand over all ammunition except that on the person to the relieving Units.

Billets 4. The 1st Seaforths and 9th Gurkhas will return to their former billets in LACOUTURE and VIEILLE CHAPELLE. Billeting Officers of 4th Seaforths and 2nd Gurkhas will report to the Staff Captain at LACOUTURE Church at 10 a.m.

Reports 5. The G.O.C Dehra Dun Bde will remain in command of the line until reliefs are completed

Issued at 7-30 p.m.

H A Walker. Major
Brigade Major Dehra Dun Bde

Copy No 1 & 2. War Diary
" " 3. Meerut Division
" " 4. Garhwal Bde
" " 5. 1st Seaforths
" " 6. 4th Seaforths
" " 7. 9th Gurkhas (who will communicate necessary orders to 4th Cavalry M.G. Detachment
" " 8. 2nd Gurkhas (who will communicate necessary orders to 107th Pioneer M.G. Detachment)
" " 9. 128 I.F.A.
" " 10. 19 BFA
" " 11. No 2 Coy Meerut Train.
" " 12. No 3 Coy S & M.

*X (c) No 3 Coy S and M will stand fast and come under orders of GOC Garhwal Bde

1. The Garhwal Bde is relieving Dehra Dun Bde tomorrow - 4th.

2. The Bn. on relief will move to its previous billets in Vieille Chapelle via Rue des Berceaux & Richebourg St Vaast.

3. The Coy. of the 4th Seaforths will rejoin their Battn. on relief.

4. Detachment M/c guns of D.D. Bde. will be relieved by guns of the Garhwal Bde. The 4th Cavalry Detacht will hand over its guns to the relieving Detacht of Garhwal Bde. and on relief will march independently to Vieille Chapelle to the G.G. billets. Horses & transport will be sent on morning 5th inst to G.G. H. Quarters at V.C. - when detacht will rejoin its unit.

5. Relieving Units will arrive at Bn H.Q about 6.45 pm.
The No 1 Coy, 4th Seaforths will be relieved by 1/6th G.
No 2 " 9th G. " " " 1/39th.
" 3 & 4 Coy (less 2 platoons) " " " Leicesters
" 1 & 2 platoons No 4. Coy " 5. 4 Bdet

6. Representatives of 1 man from each Bllet occupied by 4th Seaforths, No 2 Coy 9th G. No 3 Coy G & No 4 Coy 9th G (2 Platoons) to be at Bn H.Q. at 5.30 pm sharp. - to lead relieving units up.-
Coy Comdrs. will have ready at their own H.Q. in Rue de Bois. 4 representative guides to lead reliefs of each pl of the front line to their positions.-

"A" Form. — war diary — Army Form C.2

MESSAGES AND SIGNALS.

This message is on a/c of: **APPENDIX B**

TO: D | D | BDE

Sender's Number	Day of Month	In reply to Number	
16 R.	4th		AAA

PROGRESS REPORT C2.
RIGHT SUB-SECTION.
PICQUETS report that the water in the trenches is gradually going down but there are still from two to three feet of water and mud in fire trench of No 3 picquet. Sandbags were sent out to improve fire trenches of picquets. Loopholing of houses was carried on. Bridges across staked paths will be improved.

CENTRE AND LEFT SECTIONS
Heavy outbursts of rifle fire at 12. midnight and 4. a.m.
A machine gun was located during the day and fire brought to bear on it after dark with no appreciable result. Work

"A" Form. Army Form C. 2121.

MESSAGES AND SIGNALS.

continued on horses in Rue du Bois
and new trenches. Shelter pits
have also been dug behind
horse horses. no change in
General Situation.

From Comdg ~~~~ Pinkham

war diary
Appendix B.

Operation Orders by Lt Col G.T. Widdicombe
Commanding C2 section.

Ref. map. 1/40,000

4th Feb. 1915.

1. The Garhwal Brigade is relieving the Dehra Dun Brigade to-day.

2. The Baton on relief will move to its previous billets in VIELLE CHAPELLE via Rue de BERCEAUX and RICHEBOURG ST. VAAST.

3. The Company of the 4th SEAFORTHS will rejoin their Baton on relief.

4. Machine guns of Dehra Dun Brigade will be relieved by guns of the GARHWAL Brigade.

   Pending further orders. The 4th Cavalry Detachment will hand its guns over to the relieving detachment of GARHWAL Brigade, and on relief will march independently to VIELLE CHAPELLE to the 9th Gurkha Billets — Horses and transport will be sent on morning 5th inst to 9th Gurkha Headquarters at VIELLE CHAPELLE where detachment will rejoin its unit.

5. Relieving units will arrive at Baton Hd Qrs about 5.45 pm.
   The Coy. 4th SEAFORTHS will be relieved by 1/39 GARHWALS.
   No 2 coy 9th Gurkhas ———————————— 1/39 "
   No 3 and 4 coy (less 2 platoons) ———— Leicestershire Regt.
   15 and 16 platoons No 4 coy ———————— "

6. Representatives of one man from each billet occupied by 4th SEAFORTHS — NO 2 Coy 9th Gurkhas NO 3 Coy 9th G.R. — NO 4 Coy 9th G.R. (2 platoons) to be at BN Hd Qrs at 5.30 pm sharp to lead relieving units up.
   Coy Commanders will have ready at their own Hd Qrs in Rue du BOIS — guides to lead relief of each picquet of the front line to their positions.

(9th S.R.)

7. On relief Company Commanders will march their companies to VIELLE CHAPELLE independently and by route given in para 2 above.
The 2 platoons No 4 Coy, if still in reserve on completion of relief will be under the command of Captain PIKE.

8. Company Commanders will report at Batn Hd Qrs on completion of their relief.

9. All bombs, rifle grenades, VERY pistol Amn (not pistols themselves) and gum boots will be handed over to relieving units, receipts should be taken for numbers of pairs of gum boots and handed over by Company Commanders. Braziers taken in by companies will be brought away.
All entrenching tools will be brought away.

10. Machine guns on relief will be man handled to corner of CN. Rue des BERCEAUX (Sq. S.8.B) where they will meet their mules.

Circulated to
Comdg Coy Seaforths
O.C. 4th Cav detachment.
Comdg Coys. 9th S.R.

AAMackenzie Capt 4th Sea Hrs
GHorton Lft

11.15 am
4.2.15

JR Shepland
Capt
Adjt / 9th S.R.

O.C. to Leadhills Coy
4th Cavalry Bedds.
Coy Commander
7th G.R.

Returned to Adjutant
9th G.R.
NB Chamberlain
Major
4.ii.14

War Diary

Operation Order No 17.
by
Brigadier General C.W. Jacob
Commanding Dehra Dun Brigade

Copy No 5

LA COUTURE 7th February 1915.

Reference Map FRANCE (BETHUNE) 1/40.000.

Information 1. The SIRHIND Brigade is to relieve the DEHRA DUN Brigade on the 8th February 1915, and the latter is to move into billets South West of CALONNE.

Orders to Troops. 2. Units will pass the starting point, the cross roads in Square R.28.d. as under :— route FOSSE — LA CROIX MARMUSE — LE CORNET MALO.

Brigade Head Quarters :—	11 am	
4th Seaforths :—	11-10 am.	With Transport
9th Gurkhas :—	11-30 am.	
1st Seaforths :—	11-50 am.	
2nd Gurkhas :—	12-10 pm.	
2 Ambulance wagons 128 SFA :—		

Billeting Areas 3. 4th Seaforths will be billetted roughly in Squares Q 9, 14, 15, 20 and 21.
9th Gurkhas :— PACAUT and Q 23 a c QUENTIN Q 16.d.
1st Seaforths :— about RIEZ-DU-VINAGE (Q 26).
2nd Gurkhas :— Squares Q 27, 28 and 34.
No 2 Company Train :— CALONNE (S.W).

Billeting Officers to report to Capt WICKS, 1st Seaforths at Road junction square Q 30.a.2.2. at 9 am.

Reports 4. Brigade Head Quarters will be established in house Square Q 9.b.5.9.

H.Walker
Issued at 10.30 am.   Brigade Major Dehra Dun Brigade.

Copy No 1 and 2 War Diary   Copy No 5 9th Gurkhas   Copy No 8. 19 BFA
Copy No 3 1st Seaforths   Copy No 6 2nd Gurkhas   Copy No 9 Meerut Div
Copy No 4 4th Seaforths   Copy No 7. 128 SFA   Copy No 10. 2 Coy Train

OPERATION ORDER No. 18   Copy No. 6
                    by
         Brigadier-General C.W. Jacob.
         Commanding Dehra Dun Brigade.   CALONNE. 20th Feb. 1915

Reference.- Map FRANCE-BETHUNE 1/40,000.

Information. 1. (a) The MEERUT Division is to relieve the LAHORE Division in the front line on the 21st February and subsequent days.

(b) The Dehra Dun Brigade is to move to LACOUTURE and VIEILLE CHAPELLE on the 22nd en route to take over the Northern Section of the front on February 23rd.

Orders to Troops. 2. (a) Units will pass the Starting point - the LE CORNET MALO cross roads (Q-28-d) in accordance with the attached march table.

(b) Transport will follow units.

(c) Units will arrange for the cyclists and scouts to keep the roads clear, sidetracking traffic, until the last unit has passed -
2nd Gurkhas - From ROBECQ to RIEZ-de-VINAGE (excel) (and)
1st Seaforths From RIEZ-de-VINAGE to the starting point.

1/4th Seaforths)   Under Scout Officer, 9th Gurkhas, from
9th Gurkhas.   )   Starting Point to the two Bridges
)   over the LAWE River in R-28-d & R-34-a.

Scouts and cyclists to report at Starting Point at 8.20 a.m.

Billeting Areas. 3. Billets in LACOUTURE and VIEILLE CHAPELLE will be the same as those occupied from February 4th to 7th.

                                        H.Walker
                                           Major
                              Brigade Major Dehra Dun Brigade.
Issued at 4 p.m.

Copy No. 1   War Diary
"   No. 2   "   "
"   No. 3   MEERUT DIVISION.
"   No. 4   1st Seaforth Highrs.
"   No. 5   1/4th Seaforth Highrs.
"   No. 6   9th Gurkhas.
"   No. 7   2nd Gurkhas.
"   No. 8   No. 2 Coy Train.
"   No. 9   128th I.F.A.   ) Advised to follow same route
"   No.10   19th B.F.A.   ) as that being taken by the Bd.

DEHRA DUN BRIGADE.

Route:- Starting point - cross roads Sqr. R20-c - road junction R21-b?h - road junction R27-a-SW - Sqr. R27-c+d.

Unit	Road to starting point	Time to pass Starting point	Remarks
B.H.Q.		8-54am	Brigadier and Staff
9th Gurkhas	Sqr. Q16-d. Q22-k-d Q27-b+d	8-55am	
Pdr. Section	QUENTIN's Hr. follow Gn. Gurkhas	9-10am	
1/Seaforths	LE CORNET MALO	9-15am	
H/Seaforths	by Q20-k. Q21-c. Q27-a- to LE CORNET	9-30am	
	MALO		
2nd Gurkhas	MAROUIS - PONTLEVIS F36-a. road junction Q31-c-SW - Sqr. Q31-NC and d. - R35-a. - RUEZ-du-VINAGE - LE CORNET MALO	9-45am	Route to starting point to be reconnoitred. Any more diversions considered necessary to be reported to Bde. Headqrs. as early as possible.

1. The Meerut Div. is relieving the
   Lahore Div. in the front line on
   the 21st Feb. & subsequent days.

2. The D.O. Rde makes to Lt Couture &
   Vieille Chapelle on the 22nd & are respbe
   to Dep. over the Northern Section of the
   front on 23rd.

3. The Batt. will parade at 8.35 a.m.
   [illegible] 22nd inst. ready to march off in
   full [leaven?].

   [Transport?] will [illegible] and be ready
   at [illegible] of Kitchens — to be [illegible]
   (allocated) by the QM at the Q. Gd. Farm
   ready to [illegible] off at 8.40 a.m. & will
   follow the Batt. All bagg. will be loaded up
   by 8.35 a.m.

4. The Batt. will [pass?] the starting point at
   (9.28-d)
   the LE CORNET MALO Cross roads at
   8.55 a.m. & march via [illegible] 24 R.27-c
   junction R.27-?-1 [illegible] to Vieille Chapelle — where it
   will occupy its last billets there.

5. A big det. orderlies under Lt Kemp, will
   report at the starting point at 8.20 a.m.
   [illegible] them with the cyclists of 1/4th
   [illegible] & [illegible]. The [Batty?] will
   be responsible for keeping clear of traffic
   the road from starting point to the two
   bridges over the LAWE [river?] in R.28-c
   & R.34-a.

Operation Order No. 19

Copy No. 7.

Brigadier General A.W. Smith
Commanding Dehra Dun Bde

CALONNE 21-2-15

Information
1. (a) The Brigade is to take over the Northern Section of the line held by the Indian Corps from the Jullunder Brigade on 23rd February 1915.

(b) The Section is divided into three Sub-Sections:—
Head Quarters of Right subsection is a farm in S.8.d on ALBERT Road.
Head Quarters of Centre subsection is a house in S.9.a S.E near factory on EDWARD road.
Head Quarters of Left subsection is a farm in S.9.a.N on EDWARD road.

Order to troops.
2. (a) The 4th Seaforths will relieve the 47th Sikhs in Right Subsection.
The 2nd Gurkhas will relieve the 57th Rifles in Centre subsection.
The 1st Seaforths will relieve the Manchesters in Left subsection.

(b) Commanding Officers with two Company Commanders per battn will be at Head Quarters of the subsections they are to take over at 11 am tomorrow 22nd February to arrange details of taking over. The Jullunder Bde have issued necessary instructions to the Units of that Bde.

(c) The hours of relief on 23rd will probably be Right and Left subsections 6-15 pm. Centre subsection 7. pm. Jullunder Brigade has asked that reliefs for the picquets may arrive 20 minutes ahead of battalions.

(d) Lieut Rigby 1st Seaforths will act as Brigade Bomb gun officer and will meet the Jullunder Bomb Gun Officer at Head Quarters Left subsection at 11 am tomorrow the 22nd February.

Lt Murray
(e) Machine Gun Officers will meet the Jullunder Bde Machine Gun Officer at Head Quarters Right subsection at 10 am on 23rd February and arrange about reliefs. The distribution of guns will be approximately:—

Right Subsection — 4th Seaforths
Centre Subsection — 2nd + 9th Gurkhas.
Left Subsection — 1st Seaforths and 4th Cavalry.

In the absence of the Machine Gun Officer 4th

EW 836/4
22.2.15

4th Cavalry the Machine Gun Officer 1st Seaforths will make arrangements and inform the Gunner whose Section is under orders to report at Head Quarters Left-on-section at 6 pm on 23rd.

(4). The 7th Gurkhas will be in Brigade Reserve in RICHEBOURG ST VAAST West of Church and will take over billets at 2 pm on 23rd from 59th Rifles.

Roads 3. Units of the Brigade will use the road South of the LAWE River when moving up to RICHEBOURG ST VAAST.

Transport 4. Transport of 2nd and 7th Gurkhas will be billetted in farm COUR ST VAAST. Transport of the 1st and 4th Seaforths will take over billets now occupied by Transport of Manchesters and 47th Sikhs respectively. Baggage wagons and horses will be returned to train on 23rd February.

Ammunition 5. Units will carry 200 rounds per rifle on the man. and will take over reserve ammunition, bombs, grenades etc from relieved Units.

Reports 6. The G.O.C. Jullundur Bde will remain in Command of the line till reliefs are completed.

Dehra Dun Brigade Head Quarters will be established in same locality as before in RICHEBOURG ST VAAST.

T. N. Walker
Major.
Brigade Major Dehra Dun Brigade.

Issued at 4 pm.

Copy 1+2   Retained
Copy 3   Jullundur Bde
Copy 4   Meerut Division
Copy 5   1st Seaforths
Copy 6   4th Seaforths
Copy 7   9th Gurkhas
Copy 8   2nd Gurkhas
Copy 9   2 Company Train
Copy 10   128 F.A
Copy 11   19 B.F.A.

121/6/15.

Dehra Dunn

WAR DIARY
of
1/9th Gurkha Rifles

From Feb 27th 1915 to 27th March 1915

Pages 38-49.

Army Form C. 2118.

38

WAR DIARY
or
INTELLIGENCE SUMMARY.

(Erase heading not required.)

Instructions regarding War Diaries and Intelligence Summaries are contained in F. S. Regs., Part II, and the Staff Manual respectively. Title pages will be prepared in manuscript.

Hour, Date, Place.	Summary of Events and Information	Remarks and references to Appendices.
BILLETS RICHEBOURG ST WAAST		
FEB. 27th 1915. 4.30 pm	Orders received from Brigade to relieve one company of 1st Seaforths in the front line to light. Capt. PIKE and No1 Coy started off to relieve the company of 1st Seaforths in the trenches, and do Bais.	2 men wounded in last nights digging party.
FEB 28. 6.30 pm	Men in trenches relieved 2-7 G.R. No 2 Coy and were led by guides from 2nd G.R. to their respective positions	2 men wounded in Billets — see M.O.
7 pm	No 2 Coy relieved No1 Coy and were led up to trenches	
7.15 p	No1 Coy reached Hd Qrs and were taken up to their huts.	
8.15 p	Relief completed.	
MARCH 1st 8 am	Night fine but strong wind. Heavy rain. Quiet night.	
2 pm	Snowstorm	
3 pm	O.C. 4th SUFFOLKS came up to inspect line. Received orders for relief on night of 2nd/3rd March. Quiet night.	
MARCH 2nd	Received orders that we should be relieved by 58. Rifles in place of SUFFOLKS March pris of 2-8 G.R. bills in B direction	

WAR DIARY or INTELLIGENCE SUMMARY

Army Form C. 2118.

1/9 GR

39

Hour, Date, Place.	Summary of Events and Information	Remarks and references to Appendices.
TRENCHES RUE DU BOIS "B" SUBSECTION MARCH 2nd (continued)	Strength of the 58th Rifles (came up 15 minutes late) in front line.	
6.30 p	Maxims came of 2-9 GR to return in line.	
	Guides from Jagaits in front line arrived at No 6 Co.	
1 pm	Men for fatigues from 58th Rifles and Royal Highlanders reached the Coy and were taken up by guides to the front line.	
7.45	Coys for front line came up at 10 minutes interval and were lead up to front line. Relief completed.	
	On night 149 men chose back to man old trench in the trees avenue VIEILLE CHAPELLE.	One man wounded
Billets VIEILLE CHAPELLE MARCH 3rd	7.45 p	Carrying party of 260 men under Lt BERRY detailed to work behind RUE DU BOIS	One man wounded
MARCH 4th		Coy parades	
	7.45 p	Carrying party of 360 men under Lt KEMP detailed for work in RUE DU BOIS.	One man wounded

WAR DIARY
or
INTELLIGENCE SUMMARY.

Army Form C. 2118.

1/9 GR

(Erase heading not required.)

Instructions regarding War Diaries and Intelligence Summaries are contained in F. S. Regs., Part II, and the Staff Manual respectively. Title pages will be prepared in manuscript.

Hour, Date, Place.	Summary of Events and Information	Remarks and references to Appendices.
BILLETS VIELLE CHAPELLE		
MARCH 5th 7.12 am	Coy. parades	
6.	Coy. parades	
7.	300 men under Lt Murray detailed as working party. Coy parades.	
	300 men under Capt Price went out as covering party for work behind Rue du Bois.	
8th 10 am	Coy parades. Rapid marching	
3 pm	" " " Physical drill - bride burning	
4.15	Carrying party of 320 men detailed to work behind Rue du Bois under Captain Heatherson.	
9th 10 am	Coy parades Aircraft formation	
3 pm	10 u. k/s staged in LA COUTURE (THEATRE)	
	1 W.O. silent 1 leaked but in 10 rops. wagons.	
	Yesterday one of our aeroplanes came down in a field near Bethune huts. 1 N.C.O and 3 men detailed to guard it from 7pm No to say.	
5 pm	Rumour confirmed re our G.A.1 at the [ ] intended for 10.5 howrs would most probably come.	
7.30 pm	Received orders to move out to RICHEBOURG ST VAAST 3 am	
10.3.15	out an officer & R. Hd Qrs HdQ LA COUTURE La Couture to	

Army Form C. 2118.

WAR DIARY
or
INTELLIGENCE SUMMARY.
(Erase heading not required.)

Hour, Date, Place.	Summary of Events and Information	Remarks and references to Appendices.
Billet VIELLE CHAPELLE 10th March 1915		
3 a.m.	The Battⁿ moved from VIELLE CHAPELLE to Redoubt A.1. via RICHBOURG ST VAAST & Road through Sq.S.2.c. EDWARD Road and FORESTER LANE	
5.30 a.m.	Battⁿ Concentrated in Redoubt A.1.	
7.30 a.m.	Bombardment of NEUVE CHAPELLE commenced by the guns	
8.5 a.m.	GARHWAL Bde assaulted GERMAN trenches	
11 a.m.	The Battⁿ moved out of Redoubt A.1. and assembled in the trenches held by 6th Jats, the Head of the Battⁿ being at the Junction of the ESTAIRE - LA BASSÉE Road and Road leading to NEUVE CHAPELLE Sq S.4.c.	
4 p.m.	The following order was received from the Bde. DEHRA DUN Bde will advance on BOIS DE BIEZ and make good the road on Western edge before advancing further again. 9th GOORKHAS will direct with left	

WAR DIARY
or
INTELLIGENCE SUMMARY.

Army Form C. 2118.

(Erase heading not required.)

42

Hour, Date, Place.	Summary of Events and Information	Remarks and references to Appendices.
10.15 March 1915	on have Sqn SSM Nº 4 thence on Cross Roads S6a 5/9 right directed on road junction S5d SE and 2nd GOORKHAS to prolong line to right to Cross remainder of BOIS DE BIEZ a.a. 45 Seaforths will have half a Battn in rear of each GURKHA Battn in support and one Battn JULLUNDUR Bde will be in Echelon behind our Right flank and one Battn (R.I.A'S) in Battn Comn of that Battn to get Bridges from R.E. Report area to Supporting Battn in 45 Seaforths. (time 3.45pm)	
4.30 pm	The Battn moved out of 16 Jat trench along the road to NEUVE CHAPELLE. This was delayed as the Seaforths were moving out to attack another portion of GERMAN trench	
5pm	Head of Battn deployed from under cover of Orchard Sq S4 t 98. and 300x short of the village in a direction half left	

Army Form C. 2118.

43.

WAR DIARY
or
INTELLIGENCE SUMMARY.

(Erase heading not required.)

Instructions regarding War Diaries and Intelligence Summaries are contained in F. S. Regs., Part II, and the Staff Manual respectively. Title pages will be prepared in manuscript.

Hour, Date, Place.	Summary of Events and Information.	Remarks and references to Appendices.
10th March 1915 5.30 p.m.	Enemy had a supporting lines close of the fourth German line. Strong MG. right on to the BOIS DE BIEZ	
Dusk	Nos 1 & 2 Coys reached R. LAYES. Nos 3 & 4 Companies came up on the right to join up with 2/2 G.R. No 3 Coy reached West Edge of BOIS DE BIEZ Captured 7 Germans and Keeds.	Casualties during advance slight
8 p.m.	Line withdrawn to Right Bank of R. LAYES and consolidated.	
11th March 1915 2 a.m.	Party of Germans attempted to get round left flank of Battn. They were stopped by M.G. + Rifle fire	Several German corpses seen in front of our trenches later
7 a.m.	Received order to attack BOIS DE BIEZ when 8th Divn came up on our right.	
10 a.m.	Received message that German Counter Attack was very determined and to be ready to push forward with 8th Divn	

Gulab Singh & Sons, Calcutta—No. 22 Army C.—5-8-14—1,07,000.

Army Form C. 2118.

WAR DIARY
or
INTELLIGENCE SUMMARY.

(Erase heading not required.)

Instructions regarding War Diaries and Intelligence Summaries are contained in F. S. Regs., Part II, and the Staff Manual respectively. Title pages will be prepared in manuscript.

44

Hour, Date, Place.	Summary of Events and Information.	Remarks and references to Appendices.
11th March 1915	Our Heavy Guns bombarded German trenches to our front. Heavy German bombardment then traversed ground apparently for no effect.	
2 pm		
3.30 pm	Captain Stephens killed.	
6 pm	Received orders that the Battn would be relieved and to send an Officer to Bde HQrs to direct on relief.	Casualties during 10/11/12 March 1915 all Ranks Wounded 84
9 pm	Lieut Popden went to Bde HQrs to direct on relief, but returned with instructions that the Batt would not be relieved, but was to remain in the position they occupied with its ammunitions, stores etc.	Killed 54 (including Capt Stephens) Slightly wounded 2 (remained on duty) 17 Total 157 all Ranks
12th March 1915		
12 Mid Day	The Batt: Commenced its withdrawal.	
3 am	The withdrawal was completed.	
7 am	Last Company reached Billets at VIEILLE CHAPELLE.	

Gulab Singh & Sons, Calcutta—No. 22 Army C.—5-4-14—1,07,000.

Army Form C. 2118.

45

WAR DIARY
or
INTELLIGENCE SUMMARY.

(Erase heading not required.)

Instructions regarding War Diaries and Intelligence Summaries are contained in F.S. Regs., Part II, and the Staff Manual respectively. Title pages will be prepared in manuscript.

Hour, Date, Place.	Summary of Events and Information	Remarks and references to Appendices
12th March 1915 8:30 a.m.	The Battn marched to Billets from VIELLE CHAPELLE to LES LOBES	
10:30 a.m.	The Battn reached LES LOBES and went into Billets after some delay, waiting for billets to	
noon 4:30 p.m.	be evacuated G.O. of 28 men under Major Bates from Hospital. Reserve orders to march as soon as possible	Gen'l Bhanker Bhandari
6:30 p.m.	to RICHEBOURG ST VAAST. The Brigade being Reserve. The Battn marched to RICHEBOURG ST VAAST via LE LOBES + LA COUTURE and went into	
8:30 p.m.	billets in RICHEBOURG in front of the Church Reached near Billets	
13th March 1915	Capt Heylmour toady Ethier from Redoubt A. and buried at the Cemetery LE TOURET by Revt Dist Chaplain (Rev Danm) Grave No 18 in Row	Application has been written 20. Grave No 18 in Row.
2:30 p.m.	Revre orders to march to Billets in VIEILLE CHAPELLE	
4:15 p.m.	The Battn marched from RICHEBOURG ST VAAST	

Army Form C 2118.

WAR DIARY
or
INTELLIGENCE SUMMARY.

(Erase heading not required.)

Instructions regarding War Diaries and Intelligence Summaries are contained in F. S. Regs., Part II, and the Staff Manual respectively. Title pages will be prepared in manuscript.

46

Hour, Date, Place.	Summary of Events and Information	Remarks and references to Appendices.
13th March 1915 4.45 pm	The Battn. received VIELLE CHAPELLE and received verbal orders from Staff Captain of the Bde. to march to new formed Reserve at LES LOBES	
5.45 pm 7 pm	Reached new Billets. Reserve orders to be ready to turn out at short notice in case the Germans make a Counter Attack during the night	
LES LOBES 14th March 1915 12 noon	Draft of 1 Gurkha Officer and 158 men of the Regt. 2 Burma Military Police arrive	from BHAGSAR Rai
15th March 1915 9.15 am 3 pm	The Battn. inspected in Quarter Column by L.Genl Sir J Anderson Comdg. Corps. present Dist. Commander. Parade to new Reinforcement under Platoon Commanders. Rifle Exercises and Extended Drill	new Draft Forming 2 Companies in new
16th March 1915 10 am 2 pm 4 pm	Parade to new Reinforcements under Platoon Comdrs. Route March & Extended Drill Orders received to take command of 1/4 Gr Major Lt B Champion. New Reinforcements under Platoon Comdg. To W F Gates arrived from LA COUTURE	

Gulab Singh & Sons, Calcutta—No. 22 Army—2-5-9-11—1,07,000.

Army Form C. 2118.

47

WAR DIARY
or
INTELLIGENCE SUMMARY.

(Erase heading not required.)

Instructions regarding War Diaries and Intelligence Summaries are contained in F. S. Regs., Part II and the Staff Manual respectively. Title pages will be prepared in manuscript.

Hour, Date, Place.	Summary of Events and Information	Remarks and references to Appendices.
LES LOBES		
17th March 1915	Parade for Inspection by Lt Gen Sir James Willcocks	
11.30 a.m.	Capt H+ Ainsworth 1/10 G.R. joins Batt.	
	Capt A.E.C. St G. Gore 2/9 G.R. joins Batt.	
3 p.m.	New Reinforcements joined, composed of invalids Return Car [?]	
	and Rifle Exercises for [illegible] Drill	
4 p.m.	10 men rejoin from Hospital	
18th August 1915	Company Parades under Coy Comdrs	
10 am	Parade for Reinforcements under Platoon Comdrs	
3 p.m.		
4 pm	5 men rejoin Batt. from Hospital	
19th March 1915	Parade under Company Comdrs	
10 a.m.		
3 p.m.	Recce in the [illegible] Coy Commander	
2.3.15	Lt. H. THOMSON joined Batt for duty	
20th March 1915	Parade under Company Commanders. Rifle Exercise	
10 am + 3 pm		
	Maj. G.R. NATION joins the Batt for duty	
21st March 1915	Route Parade by Companies to check S.A. Am. on	
10 a.m	charge of Batt.	
11.30 am	Reinforcement of 1 I.G.O. + 92 Riflemen for Batt. from 1st Indian Gen[?]	

Army Form C. 2118.

48

WAR DIARY
or
INTELLIGENCE SUMMARY.
(Erase heading not required.)

Instructions regarding War Diaries and Intelligence Summaries are contained in F. S. Regs., Part II, and the Staff Manual respectively. Title pages will be prepared in manuscript.

Hour, Date, Place.	Summary of Events and Information	Remarks and references to Appendices.
LES LOBES 22nd March 1915 10 a.m.	Company Parades under Company Comdrs. her Day. Drum & Military Police Reinforcements inspected by C.O. supplied by Regt. hearts - Spoken and	
3 p.m.	Signalling L.C.O. & Stretcher-bearers Parades under Coy. Comdrs.	
23rd March 1915 10 a.m.	Comdrs Officers attended conference of Coy. and Brigade at Bn. H.Q.	
10 a.m. & 3 p.m.	Parades under Company Comdrs.	
11.30 a.m.	Reserve Ammunition shifted from Barn to heavy Shelter	
4 p.m.	Park - Called into Beaulieu from Barn of Stone under	
	Guard 7 N.C.Os & Riflemen.	
24th March 1915 8 a.m.	The Battn. marched at 8 a.m. to new billeting area	
8 a.m.	Passing Old Road Junction by R170 2£H0BES the Junction	
	Point at 8.30 a.m. Route - VIEILLE CHAPELLE - Cross Roads	
	R.182 - Road Junction R.186.	
10 a.m.	Battn. harnessed in Julien at BOUT DEVILLE by R.188.	
2.30 p.m.	Further march between Battn. and Battery billets at	
	BOUT DEVILLE Roads Drewn up; 1 yd of all	
7 p.m.	Battn. Landed to Reiets at CROIX BARBEE. S/M + C.	

Army Form C. 2118.

WAR DIARY
or
INTELLIGENCE SUMMARY.
(Erase heading not required.)

Instructions regarding War Diaries and Intelligence Summaries are contained in F. S. Regs., Part II, and the Staff Manual respectively. Title pages will be prepared in manuscript.

Hour, Date, Place.	Summary of Events and Information	Remarks and references to Appendices.
RUE DU PUITS CROIX-BARBÉ 24th-2nd March 1915.	Batt: billeted at CROIX-BARBÉ	
25th March 1915. 9.30 pm	Men K.C. in litres to consist of 1 Blanket, 1 Waterproof sheet, 1 Shirt, 1 Jersey, 1 pair of Socks, a change of Underwear. Remainder stored at LES LOBES to be sent later to billets.	
10 am	Fatigues to clear Road ditches to improve water flow	
4 pm	Party of 1 G.O. & 40 men sent to HQ by 5 pm then on ESTAIRE LA BASSÉE to fetch 200 sandbags for 2nd Gurkhas	For 2nd Gurkhas HQ.
7 pm	1 B.O. and 100 men on a fatigue to 2nd Gurkhas for day.	
26th March 1915.	1 B.O. and 100 men on fatigue to 2nd Gurkhas to dig communication trench	
10 am		Lt. TAYLOR to Convalescent
	Men fatigue. Picking up ??? officers carry ??? and ladders to 2nd Gurkha HQ.	
27th March 1915. 10 am	Fatigues to clear up ditches, improve water flow. Billeting area	Lt. Kent to Convalescent
7.30 pm	Commanding Officer and 2 Coy Commanders went 2 Gurkha trenches preparing to take over then took Subaltern & Southern Section	
7.45 pm	1 B.O. and 150 men to dug-out fatigue to 2nd Gurkhas to complete communication trench 21-39	Capt. S. ??? to Convalescent
8.30 pm	??? and Batt. HQ. Remainder going up into line S.Staff B	

121/b1/15

WAR DIARY
of
1/9th Gurkha Rifles

From 28th March 1915 to 30th April 1915

Pages 50 to 64.

Army Form C. 2118.

WAR DIARY
or
INTELLIGENCE SUMMARY.

(Erase heading not required.)

Instructions regarding War Diaries and Intelligence Summaries are contained in F.S. Regs., Part II, and the Staff Manual respectively. Title pages will be prepared in manuscript.

50

Hour, Date, Place.	Summary of Events and Information	Remarks and references to Appendices.
Rue du Puits CROIX BARBEE 28th March		
6.45 p.m.	Sent to Support HQrs No 4 Coy for Search Party and Bridges during afternoon to take up to Trenches.	Capt Ainsworth + No 2 Coy
	No 3 Coy with 2 Platoons No 1 Coy and Head Qrs march to relieve 2nd Gurkhas in Front Line Route via PONT LOGI. No 3 Coy with 2 Platoons of No 1 Coy form Firing Line and Support to Right Subsector	
6.55 p.m.	No 4 Coy with 1 Platoon No 1 Coy to relieve Left Subsector but have followed wrong Party by same Route.	
7.5 p.m.	No 2 Coy with Remaining Platoon No 1 Coy follow Reserve path to Relieve 2nd Gurkha Reserves	
10.0 p.m.	Relief of Subsector "B" Southern Section completed. Work commenced on completion of Relief to improve Communicator Trenches & Fire trenches, and build a parados.	Casualties - Nil
29th March	1/2 G.R. Machine Guns remain in trench with panadoo. During early hrs of morning some German Dead in front our Trenches were buried, also an Officer of a British Regt. identification unknown was buried. Lieut Renshaw and Naik Bar? Pahan sent to Brigade. Capt Walkman suffering from sore eye went back to 1st line Transport. Capt Gunn took command of No 4 Coy	
6 p.m.		

WAR DIARY
or
INTELLIGENCE SUMMARY.

(Erase heading not required.)

Army Form C. 2118.

Hour, Date, Place.	Summary of Events and Information	Remarks and references to Appendices.
Trenches B Southern Section 29th March 1915. 8.30 pm	Working parties of 150 men from 2nd Gurkhas with 1/o of Reserve Company under Capt Ainsworth and Lt Taylor back on Right and Left Communication Trenches. Right Com: Trench completed. Bridges & Blinds got up to cross drains, and bridges deficient with Sandbag Barricades. Parados in front being continued.	Casualties - 1 Killed, 1 Wounded
30th March 1915	During early hours of morning, Germans fired in four song(?) of parapet of Left Subsector. Our Working Party, which were being withdrew. Germans fired on, and sent to Bugero. Our Machine Gun fire on German working parties. Heavy machine gun fire all night.	
9 am	Hostile aeroplane appeared our lines, but retired on our anti gun opening fire	
11.30 am	Col Charles (Naser Corp Staff) visited our lines	
6.30 pm	apptd Capt Matheson & Lieut Kemp Moulded in 7 Chapa trees German Trench K.Z. 14 fired by Lt Taylor and to Bryan Rifle grenade 2 in duds with anxiety in German Brentwork in front of our Left Subsector	
7.30 pm	Capt AINSWORTH left Jufferr 75 Rifles at Road Junction M.27.D and conducted them to Bois Grenier	

Army Form O. 2118.

WAR DIARY
or
INTELLIGENCE SUMMARY.
(Erase heading not required.)

52

Hour, Date, Place.	Summary of Events and Information	Remarks and references to Appendices.
TRENCHES, Sub-Sector "B" Southern Section, NEUVE CHAPELLE. 30th March 1915. 8 p.m.	Officers of 57th Rifles relieving unit go round trenches with officers of Coy: Trenches found not by Reserve Company. Enemy trenches improved. Heavy machine gun fire all night.	Casualties - 1 Wounded
31st March 1915.	German Artillery more active than usual.	
	2nd Lieut Bell proceeds on 7 days leave. Lieut Poynder goes sick. Lt Joyce takes over duties as Quartermaster.	
5 p.m.	German aeroplane flying low is an enemy direction passes over Battn H.Q.	
5.30 p.m.	Batt: Gun battery bombard German trenches in front of Rifles Sub Sector.	
7.30 p.m.	Capt Ancourtt meets relieving unit at Road Junction M.72 and conducts it to Batt: H.Q.	
8 p.m.	Relief of Left Subsector arrives at Batt: H.Q.	
8.30 p.m.	Relief of Right Subsector arrives at Batt: H.Q.	
10.30 p.m.	Relief of Batt: completed. Companies marched to VIELLE CHAPELLE via Road Junction M.73 - Road Junction M.32.b - Road Junction M.26.c. independently.	
	It is to be regretted that no opportunity was found during the period in the line of testing the fighting qualities and value of the Reinforcements from the Police Batt.	Committee one

Army Form C. 2118.

WAR DIARY
or
INTELLIGENCE SUMMARY.
(Erase heading not required.)

Instructions regarding War Diaries and Intelligence Summaries are contained in F. S. Regs., Part II, and the Staff Manual respectively. Title pages will be prepared in manuscript.

53

Hour, Date, Place.	Summary of Events and Information	Remarks and references to Appendices.
VIELLE CHAPELLE 1st April 1915 2 am	The Battn arrived in its old billets at VIELLE CHAPELLE. Odd A.T. Mule carts attached to stores	
4 hrs.	The Battn moved to billets at CROIX MARMUSE	
6 hrs.	The Battn Billeted here. Transport carts arrived to replace its A.T. Carts previous to moving from VIELLE CHAPELLE	
2nd April 1915 2.30 pm	Morning spent in cleaning up Battn Parade to prevent Htrs Paurkhis Mule with the G.O.C. had no promoted by his Regim: mother of Lce Naik L.C.C. Rogers	
4 hrs.	Lt Poynter resigned + taken over duty of Quartermaster	
3rd April 1915 10 am	L.G.C. D.C. inspects kast Reinforcement of M.G.S Police and were taught for duty in front line	1 G.O. + 92 men
10am 12 noon 3-4 pm 4.30 pm	Company parades under Capt. Coms. Specially for musketry and temps of M.C. Police Requirements Football match with 1/4 Seaforths Result Draw 3–3	
4th April 1915 10 April 1915	Lt Col Wadmore and Lt Murray proceed on leave to	
5th April 1915 6 " " 7 " " 8 " " 9 " "	Battn = Rests in Billets. Parades daily under Coy Com'drs From 10 am till noon + from 3–4 pm. Battn Route march on 6th April to MERVILLE.	

WAR DIARY
or
INTELLIGENCE SUMMARY.
(Erase heading not required.)

Army Form C. 2118.

524.

Hour, Date, Place	Summary of Events and Information	Remarks and references to Appendices
CROIX MARMUSE 10th April 1915 4 p.m.	Inspection of Brigade by Field Marshal Sir John French, Comd in Chief at LESTREM.	
11th April 1915 10 a.m.	C.O., Adjt & Company Commanders meet O.C. 2nd Inf[try] Bn at Bn H.Qrs. in Richebourg ST VAAST, and go to see trenches, meeting guides at Road Junction M.27.D. and going round section to be taken over	Capt Gore acts as interpreter to 2nd GR and the Batt⁵. Lt Willshire & Lt Munro return from leave
6.45 p.m.	Batt⁵ H.Q., Right Half Batt⁵, machine guns and 1st line transport move to trenches to relieve 2nd Royal Sussex Reg⁵.	
7.15 p.m.	Left Half Batt⁵ move to trenches. Route taken via Road Junction R.20.c. ZELOBES - VIEILLE CHAPELLE - BOUT DEVILLE - PONT DU HEM 3 minute interval observed between Companies from PONT DU HEM.	
9.15 p.m.	Met Guides at Road Junction M.27.D, 1 Company to support No 3 Coy Right No 1 Coy Reserves No 14 Coy	

Distribution of Relief:
M.G.

Army Form C. 2118.

WAR DIARY
or
INTELLIGENCE SUMMARY.
(Erase heading not required.)

55

Hour, Date, Place	Summary of Events and Information	Remarks and references to Appendices
In front of NEUVE CHAPELLE Subsector "D" 12th April 1915	Reliefs slow as some Guides failed to find Companies and night was very dark.	Casualties – 3 wounded
1.30 a.m.		
3 a.m.	Relief Completed.	
	Sent up 1 Platoon of No 3 under Subr MEHAR SINGH to fill up the gap on left of No 2 Coy with 2 Black Watch with view to improving liaison Coy with them.	
7.30 p.m.	CHATEAU REDOUBT ammunitien with a view to being occupied. CHATEAU REDOUBT occupied by 1 Platoon holding under Jamadar Multan. Its disposition: Firing Line { Right Centre Nine No 1 Coy No 1 & No 14 Scouts Chateau Redoubt Left Major Bignell 1 Platoon No 4 Coy holding Two M.Gs. Supports 1 Platoon No 4 Coy 3 Platoon No 3 (Capt Ainsworth) Reserves 3 Platoon No 4 (Capt Hawkins)	

Army Form C. 2118.

WAR DIARY
or
INTELLIGENCE SUMMARY.
(Erase heading not required.)

56

Instructions regarding War Diaries and Intelligence Summaries are contained in F.S. Regs., Part II. and the Staff Manual respectively. Title pages will be prepared in manuscript.

Hour, Date, Place	Summary of Events and Information	Remarks and references to Appendices
Sub-Sector D. NEUVE CHAPELLE 12th April 1915	Home in NEUVE CHAPELLE reconnoitred with a view to being used as a Sniper Post. 465 Battery R.F.A. came in front.	
7 pm	Fatigue for carrying cement to 1/39 Brigade	
7.30 pm	Lt. Kemp + 50 men	
11.30 pm	Capt. Grey + 100 men	
	1/3 Rifle Bde. Reserve in front of our Report to No 1 Coy	
13th April 1915	Snipers take up position in Sniper Home	
6 am	The Brigadier goes round Subsector D	
11 am	Subr. Mohan Sing & Bhagat Bahadur leave for	
1.30 pm	Godwine Bde HQs. VIEILLE CHAPELLE to meet Lord Curzon	
	of Kedleston at 2 p.m.	
	1 Prisoner taken - came in to No 1 Coy	Casualties - 1 Wounded
10.30 pm	German artillery active - one shell hit on Battalion	Belonged to 13th Prussian Regt. 7th Coy having Jasper bay a native of Lorraine.
14 April 1915	and on left communication trench.	
1.30 pm	Sniper report enemy taking water from their trenches, & commenced to potter another	Casualties - 1 killed by rifle fire
	Snipers claim 1 German hit, but very little movement is shown. German losses	By shell - 1 wounded 1 slightly wounded

Army Form C. 2118.

WAR DIARY
or
INTELLIGENCE SUMMARY.

(Erase heading not required.)

Instructions regarding War Diaries and Intelligence Summaries are contained in F.S. Regs., Part II. and the Staff Manual respectively. Title pages will be prepared in manuscript.

Hour, Date, Place	Summary of Events and Information	Remarks and references to Appendices
Sub Section B. NEUVE CHAPELLE. 14th April 1915 7.30 pm	Working parties from No 3 Coy Canadians were left. Working Party from No 4 Coy Canadians near Guide Coy Trench. Working Party from No 1 Canadian Right Coy Trench to Surface Mine. 7 British + 3 German torpedoes fired by No 1 Coy.	
15th April 1915 2.15 pm	Hostile aeroplane attempted to come over then retired when our anticraft guns opened fire. 44th Batt'n relieved by 46th Battery covering our front. Sappers report German weaving Round Barracans + Ravensin Cuts.	Casualties 1 Killed 1 Wounded
5 pm	Enemy working parties as on 14th inst. 13 Bodies both British + German thrown by No 1 Coy. New Flare hote-lamp Searchlight tried but proved a failure.	
16th April 1915 9 am	Reconnoitred our trench + that of 2nd Bench Water with 1 Col Henry with a view to advancing portions of our line from Post 143 - to Pt 156. Reported to Brigade to be a large + difficult operation. Snipers claim 3 Germans hit. Volley of Rifle Grenades at dusk + Dawn daily at enemy parapet present no Results of none apparent	Casualties nil

WAR DIARY
or
INTELLIGENCE SUMMARY.
(Erase heading not required.)

Army Form C. 2118.

58

Hour, Date, Place	Summary of Events and Information	Remarks and references to Appendices
16th April 1915	Range chart made by Lt Mowbray with Bar & Stroud Range-finder.	
7.30 p.m.	Work done on 3 new Coms Trenches.	
11 p.m.	Patrol attempted to recover the body of a German officer but hostile trenches playing on the body prevented attempt.	
17th April 1915	CHATEAU Redoubt supplied with 3 days Water Supply and 20 hours Am̃n.	
2.30 p.m.	Lt Gen Sir C Anderson Cmdg Meerut Divn visited our lines and lunched at HQrs.	Casualties — 1 wounded accidentally by trap exploding in his hand
8 p.m.	Snipers claim 1 German hit. Machine Guns of 107th Pioneers under Capt Carlisle came into the one Gun returned 2/4th Seaforth Gun in our Right Redoubt one Gun in Chateau Redoubt. Work continued on Coms Trenches. Enemy reported to be wearing new Grey Caps.	
18th April 1915		
3.30 a.m.	No 3 Coy relieved No 1 Coy in Right Sub Sector. No 1 Coy left 1 Platoon in line on right of No 2 Coy.	Casualties — 1 Killed — 1 Slightly wounded
9.30 a.m.	Hostile aeroplane flying high went beyond our lines	
9.40 a.m.	Hostile aeroplane attacked, however men on trench it signalled by dropping smoke balls, and passed on	

Army Form C. 2118.

WAR DIARY
or
INTELLIGENCE SUMMARY.
(Erase heading not required.)

Instructions regarding War Diaries and Intelligence Summaries are contained in F. S. Regs., Part II. and the Staff Manual respectively. Title pages will be prepared in manuscript.

59

Hour, Date, Place	Summary of Events and Information	Remarks and references to Appendices
18th April 1915 4 pm 8 pm	The Brigadier visited the line. Working parties on Com? Trenches & 2" line Trenches no 4 Coy relieved no 2 Coy on left sub sector	
19th April 1915 8 pm	Work continued on com? Trenches & to improve line. Machine Gun scattered German working party killing two. The party was attempting to put up a parapet in front of their wire entanglement	Casualties - 1 wounded
20th April 1915 10 am 3.30 pm & 5 pm 9 pm	C.O. and Adj? attend conference of C.Os at Bt HQrs German Aeroplane attempted to cross our lines but turned on our anti-aircraft guns opening fire Comm. Com? Trench completed	Casualties - nil
21st April 1915	Enemy Artillery more active than usual. One direct hit by Pip Squeak on our Right Trench Parapet. Shrapnel hit up to prevent Exposure to fire on Right front. Work on 2" line & Pts Comm? Trench continued. 2" line Trench behind Redoubt Right sub sector	Casualties - nil

WAR DIARY or INTELLIGENCE SUMMARY

Army Form C. 2118.

60

Hour, Date, Place	Summary of Events and Information	Remarks and references to Appendices
22nd April 1915	C.O. and Adjt. made a reconnaissance of terrain up to Rue de Bois at Quinque.	
10 a.m.		
11 a.m.	Hostile aeroplane seen over our line, marked with small white crosses on French ground. It made off when fired on.	
4.15 p.m.	Hostile aeroplane again appeared on line but rapidly retired on being fired on.	
3 a.m.	Bouilly B'y opened rapid fire on convoy which drew a heavy rifle, trench gun, & artillery fire from Burstaden.	Casualties. 1 Wounded by rifle gun fire. 1 Killed.
8.30 p.m.	Artillery fired at P5 111 T 113 where Enemy transport had been heard. 44th Battery RFA relieved 44th Battery. Covering on that front.	
	Hqrs Left C^in^C Trench completed.	
23rd April 1915	Officer 57th Rifles not traced with a view to relieving us in.	(1) Report that German heavy 'bus Gun deepening range a then slowing artillery cavalcading in trenches. Casualties. 1 Killed/Rifle Fire.
10 a.m.	Receive news that relief has been postponed.	
4 p.m.		
23rd April 1915	Hostile Boot Gun opened fire on our left Piquet House, but was at once silenced by artillery fire.	
6 p.m.		

WAR DIARY or INTELLIGENCE SUMMARY.

(Erase heading not required.)

Army Form C. 2118.

Hour, Date, Place	Summary of Events and Information	Remarks and references to Appendices
Neuve Chapelle Sub Section D 24th April 1915 2 am	Two Premature Bursts of our Guns over Houses during Day. The work of improving the Supports was continued. Two Machine Gun Shelters located between Points 137 & 141.	Casualties – Wounded 1 by Rifle fire. Burst of our gun.
25th April 1915	Brewery heavily shelled, as shells treated on parapet. Shell considered to be 5.9" howitzer. C.O. & Adjt 2/3rd G.R. visit trenches with view to relief by Chateau Redoubt garrison (cans to 2 Platoons) [relieving] 3 Coy 2/3rd G.R. 1	Casualties Killed – 1 by Rifle fire.
26th April 1915 7 am	Supg Coy 2/3rd G.R. visit line with view to relieving us. Chateau Redoubt garrison relieved by 1 Platoon Bn [Battn] Scot Gun Detachment take up position in new Left Subsection with a view to relieving Horse Road Gun. Germans very careless in burying their dead. [illegible] stuck they not ten.	Casualties – nil Snipers & patrols very slack sniping.
27th April 1915 8 pm 10.10 pm 11 pm	Burst Gun fire from Germans at no Project [illegible] silenced by our Bomb Gun and artillery Fire. British Officers & support Coy came into A.P. Redoubt. Relief of Sub Section "D" completed. Battn [illegible] on Billets move into A.P. Redoubt & Platoons under 2nd Lt Duncan move up to Support. Finishers were G/6 McCartney	Casualties 1 Wounded by Rifle fire 2 wounded Slightly by Burst fire from Machine Gun mounted in line with Chimney.

WAR DIARY or INTELLIGENCE SUMMARY

Army Form C. 2118.

62

Hour, Date, Place	Summary of Events and Information	Remarks and references to Appendices
27th April 1915	(a) During the PERNES BOIS wood in Subsector D Centre Section, the Snipers with Telescopic Sights have claimed to obtain German hits. Rifle positions hit. They obtained useful information on enemy's work in trenches & very successfully stopped German snipers from movement behind their lines. (b) A very bitter wind along the ground unless Rifle stubble angle & checked a German Patrol which had crawled to try to L. Fr. showing that the bitter so that given the Brawny team came to take cover and not come as a gallant surprise. (c) Enemy attempted to put up pompts in front of their wire entanglement which was successfully stopped by our M.G. fire. 2 men & 1 working party were killed.	Germans seem to be shorter or in trenches you English no good
A. Report 28th April 1915 10 am	CO & OCs No 1 & 2 Coys went meet O.C. 6th Jats at their HQrs Rue du PUITS in connection with taking over Part of Southern Section ROE DE BOIS and afterwards visit trenches to be taken over from 3rd London Regt.	

Army Form C. 2118.

WAR DIARY
or
INTELLIGENCE SUMMARY.
(Erase heading not required.)

63

Hour, Date, Place	Summary of Events and Information	Remarks and references to Appendices
A.1. Redoubt 28th April 1915	Lt Gen Sir C Anderson Comdg Resrv Divn made a 1st visit to A.1 Redoubt.	
11 a.m.		
2 p.m.	A.1. Redoubt shelled by 5.9" Howitzers	1 Shell in redoubt but blind
8.15 p.m.	No 1 Coy under Capt Pike marched to take over part of Southern Section	
8.25 p.m.	No 2 Coy under Major Rynell marched to take over left portion of Southern Section. The Batt places under Comd of Col Roche C.B. Comdg 6th Jats.	Casualties } 1 Killed by Rifle fire } 1 Wounded
29th April 1915 8 p.m.	1 Peloton of No 3 Coy moved up into Redoubt. Redoubt in support.	
	Lieut R G H Murray awarded the MILITARY CROSS. Subadar Mohan Sing Khatri } awarded 1st OM 2nd Class Jem (honry Lt) Sheoboksh Lal }	Jem. Kuder Sing
9.30 p.m.	Lt Murray + No 4 Detachment returns from Subsection "D" Central Section + rejoins Batt in A.1. Redoubt.	Casualties — Nil

WAR DIARY
or
INTELLIGENCE SUMMARY.

(Erase heading not required.)

Army Form C. 2118.

64

Hour, Date, Place	Summary of Events and Information	Remarks and references to Appendices
A.I. Redoubt 30th April 1915 6 p.m. 9 p.m.	C.O. & Adjutant attend Conference of C.Os at Bn. H.Q. CROIX BARBEE Fatigue of two British Officers and 150 O.R. digging & Revt. trenches in Southern outskirts Redoubt to Rue Tilleul	Casualties - 1 wounded (Rifleman Zira) Capt Goss Lt. Kemp Duning Period 18th-27th 7 men Reposed Battn from Hospital

G.J. Willcombe
Lt Col
Comdg 1/9th Gurkha Rifles

Serial No 96.

121/5799

WAR DIARY
OF
1st Battalion 9th Gurkha Rifles.

From 1st May 1915 To 31st May 1915.

From
Officer Commanding
1/9th Goorkha Rifles   Field 6th June 15

No 13811   No 82A

To
The C. G. S.
A. H. Q.
INDIA

REC'D 2 JUL 15

I am sending herewith "WAR DIARY" from 1st May to 31st May 15 both date inclusive.

Kindly acknowledge receipt.

R. Widdicombe
Lieut Col
Commanding 1/9th G.R.

Army Form C. 2118.

65

WAR DIARY
or
INTELLIGENCE SUMMARY.
(Erase heading not required.)

Instructions regarding War Diaries and Intelligence Summaries are contained in F. S. Regs., Part II. and the Staff Manual respectively. Title pages will be prepared in manuscript.

Hour, Date, Place	Summary of Events and Information	Remarks and references to Appendices
Lansdowne Post (A.1) 1st May 19/15	Heavy Bombardment of Rue de Bois and support trenches up to Lansdowne Post by Germans from 4 am to 5 am. Our artillery silenced their fire. Fatigue 1/100 men on duty.	Casualties 4 wounded
4 am		
8 pm	Fatigue work of 65 Tots on communication trenches from buildings to front line.	
2nd May 19/15 8 pm	Fatigue of 70 men on improvement work in front line.	
3rd May 19/15		
10 am	Officers 2nd G.R. front line with view to relieving on	
8.10 pm	9th G.R. moving relieve 2nd G.R. M.G. in front line	
9.30 pm	Relief of Battn by 2nd G.R. commenced	
10.10 pm	Relief of Battn by 2nd G.R. completed. Battn. marched by Companies to Rue de Vieille Chapelle	
VIELLE CHAPELLE 4th May	Battn. rests in Billets	
5th May	Company Commanders to inspect kits. Item found not carried as under:—	
	* 1 Blanket 1 Waterproof sheet 1 Shirt 1 pr Socks 1 pair Pants Holdall etc	* Carried on Limbers To blankets or kits carts. Remainder on other two carts

Army Form C. 2118.

WAR DIARY
or
INTELLIGENCE SUMMARY.
(Erase heading not required.)

66

Hour, Date, Place	Summary of Events and Information	Remarks and references to Appendices
Nelle Chapelle 6th May 1915 8 am 9.30 p.m.	Fatigue of 100 men under Lieut Collins to Rue de Paris to work under Divn Signal Officer	
7th May 1915	Fatigue of 200 men under Lt Taylor & 2nd Lt Brennan to 6th Batn HQrs 96 Piccadilly to dig Communication Trenches Battn Receives orders to move to Armentry Trenches preparatory to attacking at Dawn on 8th Above orders cancelled.	
8th May 1915 1 p.m. 8.30 p.m. 8.40 p.m 8.50 " 9 p.m 11.30 p.m	Receive orders that Operation ordered for 8th would take place on 9th May HQrs and No 4 Coy march via CROIX BARBE - St VAAST Come & Indly line to take up position of assembly at Rue de BOIS in D.D.S Trenches No 3 Coy marches } Following same route as No 2 Coy marches } No 4 Coy No 1 Coy and R.Q. Head } All Battn assembled	
9th May 1915 5 a.m. 5.40 " 6.30 am	Artillery Bombardment commenced First Assault took place & resulted in a failure Left Half Battn move up to reinforce 1st Seaforths, and Right Half Battn moves up to support 4th Seaforths	

Army Form C. 2118.

WAR DIARY
or
INTELLIGENCE SUMMARY.
(Erase heading not required.)

67

Hour, Date, Place	Summary of Events and Information	Remarks and references to Appendices
RUE DE BOIS 9th May 15 7 am	1 Platoon of No 3 Coy under Lieut Ashton swing whether 1st Seaforths were over the trench parapet to support in a further assault. No 1 Coy under Capt Pike moved up to join tunnel to reinforce 4th Seaforths with No 2 Coy in support during the morning. Heavy Hostile Artillery bombardment on our line and support trenches. Heavy Casualties.	Casualties Slightly Wounded In the F.R.T. advance Killed 8 Wounded 108 Injured by Ruk T&u Shell fire 3& hernia 4 Sick 4 Slaves returned next day Total 127
11.30 am	C.O. and Adjt ordered to Bde HQrs to see Brigadier and told by Brigadier that Bn. is to be relieved at once by Bareilly Bde who went to make a further assault after a second infantry Bombardment at 3.40 p.m. The Batt. ordered to Breastwork, East of LANSDOWNE Post in reserve to Garhwal Bde.	
3.40 pm 3.50 pm 5 pm	Battn. collected in above Breastwork. Batt. ordered to follow Dehradun to Carnoustie Trenches CO and Adjt report to Garhwal Bde HQrs in Rue de Bois to receive instructions to move into Bn. trenches following the Leinsters.	
6 pm	Receive orders to rejoin Dehra Dun Bde now occupying Carr Trench and Breastwork East of LANSDOWNE POST.	

WAR DIARY or INTELLIGENCE SUMMARY

Army Form C. 2118.

68

Hour, Date, Place	Summary of Events and Information	Remarks and references to Appendices
RUE DE BOIS, 9th May 15 6.30 p.m.	Received verbal orders from Adm Div Bde to move to to billets near VIELLE CHAPELLE.	
10.30 p.m.	Battn in Billets.	
VIELLE CHAPELLE		
10th May 15	Battn not in Billets. Bde became Divisional Reserve, and Battn under orders to turn out in one hour. Parades daily under Coys.	Capt Hanney goes sick.
11th May 15	"	
12th May 15	"	
13th May 15	Sir George Willcocks visited Battn & had tea. 2/2nd Battn O'Ogilvy joined Battn (2 new (sick & wounded) Officers joined)	Capt Gilroy 1st 3 Jones Battn
14th May 15	37 men joined Battn (9 Reinforcements minus sick & wounded)	* 8 Reinforcements, 3 sick.
15th May 15	2nd Lt Battin & Ogilvy transferred to 1/8th G.R. & 11 men joined Battn	
16th May 15	Battn free in readiness to move	
4.30 a.m. 5 "	Battn fell in but remained in constant readiness to move. The Bde becomes Corps Reserve resuming a state of Readiness.	The Brigadier visited the Battn daily while in Billets
6 p.m.	Battn resumes its state of Readiness	
17th May 15	Battn remains in state of Constant Readiness and Battn remains in state of Constant Readiness	
18th May 15 9.30 a.m.	Battn moved into trenches south of RUE DU PUITS and west of CROIX BARBEE with Battn HQrs at CROIX BARBEE. Coys went to clear billets to Highland Div.	2 men moved to ZELOBES.
19th May 15	Battn remains trenches in trenches Capt Kinman IMS relieves Capt Gilroy in medical charge of Battn.	

Army Form C. 2118.

WAR DIARY
or
INTELLIGENCE SUMMARY.
(Erase heading not required.)

69

Hour, Date, Place	Summary of Events and Information	Remarks and references to Appendices
CROIX BARBEE 20th May 1915	Battⁿ remained stationary. Capt Gilroy reported sick and took over medical charge of Battⁿ from Capt Kinnear.	Major Reynold gone sick.
21st May 1915 2.30 p.m.	Battⁿ returned by Company at 15 minutes interval to Billets between VIELLE CHAPELLE + LA COUTURE	Tempy Lt Collum transferred to 39th Garhwal Rifles
4 p.m.	Battⁿ settled in Billets.	
VIELLE CHAPELLE 22nd May 23rd May 10.30 am	Battⁿ rested in Billets. C.O. attended conference of C.Os at Bde HQrs at 6 p.m. The C in C officer Adyts Compys Comdrs + machine Gun officers visited Bde H.Q. on Edward Road and went round trenches held by 4th Battn Kings Liverpool Regt preparing to relieving them	15 Sick reported from MARSEILLES 3 wounded reported of Sgt Unknown Major
6.45 p.m.	Machine Gun Detachment moved from billets to take up position in line	
7.45 p.m.	Battⁿ moved up into trenches from Billets via RICHEBOURG St VAAST and WINDY CORNER by Companies with 15 minute interval over of march No 2.1.3+4	
10.55 p.m.	Line taken over and Relief Completed. Work done to improve parapets + trenches taken over	Capt Mathewson Gunning Killed
24th May 10 a.m.	Enemy infantry sent out to bury dead between our German lines before light. Vice Brigadier got round the line Regimental inspected by stretchers	Casualties men wounded by Rifle fire

Army Form C. 2118
WAR DIARY
or
INTELLIGENCE SUMMARY.
(Erase heading not required.)

70/=

Hour, Date, Place	Summary of Events and Information	Remarks and references to Appendices
Fauches Rue de Bois	Distribution of Fancy line Supports & Reserves	
	Fancy line Supports Bor 3 + 4 Coys Reserves Bor 1 + 2 Coy	
25th May 1915 7.30 pm	Reconnaissance of ground between Ferme du Bois carried out by guiding officers, patrols take over part of new trench to left of ours out with 4th Seaforths, to take new portion of line this our night by 6th Jats. 6th Jats relieve 21st M. gordons further work carried out to improve trenches. Heavy snow trench Officers patrol movements enemy line on Patrol went Lt Kemp. commander under guided officer	Casualties - Capt Gros Slipper wounded
26th May 1915 3.45 am	Officers 2nd G.T.R. go round line preparatory to relieving Bn.2.	
am 12.30 pm	Lt Genl Sir C Anderson Comg Meerut Divn goes round the Bn 2587. Lt Col Thomson Knowers brought in a wounded man of HL.I. Lt Capt Gregg who had been lying out wounded near R.E. mine attack by Sirhind Bde on 25/27 May during period Battalion was in line, the Reserves + Communicn. trenches were constantly shelled into Chapelle + Hope Explosion Sole 2nd Gurkha Rifles were known	Casualties - nil

Army Form C. 2118.

WAR DIARY
or
INTELLIGENCE SUMMARY.
(Erase heading not required.)

7/

Hour, Date, Place	Summary of Events and Information	Remarks and references to Appendices
26th May 1915 10 p.m.	Relief of Battn by 2nd G.R. commenced	
27th May 1915 12.30 a.m.	Battn completed relief and settles in trenches and dugouts astride the Albert Road, Reserves Brigade Reserve with Battn Hd Qrs	Casualties - Brigr 2 men wounded 2 Sick reports Battn 7 pm I.F.A.
28th May 1915 10 a.m. Albert Road	Battn rests in trenches astride Albert Road.	
8 p.m.	Carrying fatigue of 150 men under Lieut Hemmings report to R.E. officer at St Vaast fort, and carry up materials to trenches near R6. Smaller fatigue of same work under Lieut Kemp of 80 men.	Casualties - nil 2 men wounded
6.30 p.m.	Visit by Brigadier	
29th May 15 10.30 am 8 p.m.	Carrying fatigue of 150 men under Capt Gow to report at St Vaast Caves to Pioneer officer for carrying to R6.	Casualties - nil 1 man accidentally cut by trenching tool. 2 Sick reports to I.F.A.
30th May 1915 3.15 pm	Co'y Officers Coy Comrs M.G. Officer + Adjutant visit line to be taken over from 8th Argylls, and get down to trenches in twelves	Trenches RB - Q7
9 p.m.	Companies march at 15 minutes interval to trenches	

Army Form C. 2118.

WAR DIARY
or
INTELLIGENCE SUMMARY.
(Erase heading not required.)

Instructions regarding War Diaries and Intelligence Summaries are contained in F.S. Regs., Part II. and the Staff Manual respectively. Title pages will be prepared in manuscript.

72

Hour, Date, Place		Summary of Events and Information	Remarks and references to Appendices
Albert Road	30th May '15 9 p.m.	No I Coy under Capt Pike with machine guns move part of many line.	1 Sick Reynolds from I.F.A
	9.15 p.m.	No II Coy under Capt Gardner to front line supports (old German front trench).	
	9.30 p.m.	No III Coy under Capt Arnimell move to 2nd line supports (as pointed out French).	
	9.45 p.m.	No IV Coy under Capt Mackinnon into Reserve Breastworks at Junction of ALBERT ROAD – RUE DE BOIS. Relief complete.	
	31st May 1915 10 a.m.	Brigadier visits HQrs and goes round the line. Shelling of trenches by Field (Pip Squeaks) and Heavy Guns continues during day and night.	Casualties – 190 Wounded (Charles of Platt, 2nd Kohlberg Bern) Wounded. 3 other rks killed 2 other rks missing 1 other rks home, returned sick 1 me on return.
	10 p.m.	Parties from No I Coy 3' out to dig advanced fire trench Q8 – Q7.	
	11 p.m.	Supports under Lieut Taylor ensuredly relieved and found to withdraw.	
	11 p.m.	No III Coy move up with some trench ers as no II Coy Capt Pike and Report Party successfully complete occupation into 1 Section in front of Q7. Front of Batt. Covered by B Batt & Part of 44th Batt, R.F.A.	2 Sick Reynolds Baker from I.F.A

Signed [illegible] Lt Col
Comdt 21/25 G.R

Serial No. 96.

121/6128

WAR DIARY
OF
1/9th Gurkha Rifles.

From 1st June 1915. To 30th June 1915.

WAR DIARY
or
INTELLIGENCE SUMMARY.
(Erase heading not required.)

Army Form C. 2118

Hour, Date, Place	Summary of Events and Information	Remarks and references to Appendices
Trenches R3-Q7. June 1st 1915. 10 am night.	During the day/night: Inspected shelling of the Fire, Support and Reserve trenches. Brigadier visited around trenches. Enemy continued and made 6 LRD/Platoon raids by day & night by 1 MG. 2nd Reserve watch & 1 Platoon, to 4 by relieves to 3 Coy in Support. Shelling not so heavy on front line. Further work carried on by Nos 1 & 2 Coy in advanced trench - completed to hold 2 platoons and also by 3 & 4 platoons in support. Listening patrols out at night to cover working parties. Distribution. Advanced trench — 2 platoon 1 MG/Rifle water 1/2 Fire trench —— 5 platoon — 2 M.G. Supports —— 3 platoon Reserve —— 1 Company 6th Tots on left. 2nd Reserve watch on Report/Bombay B" 6th Tots relieved on 2nd June by 4th Royal Fusiliers	Casualties 6 wounded by Rifle fire. 1 Sick man away from 1.F.A. 7 6.Tots take up 6. yds from no 2 Coy on left and No 2.Cy Taken over to the 2 trenches at Q7. Relieved four keepers fresh"" Casualties - 1 wounded 4 men Reports from Sick from 1F.A.

WAR DIARY or INTELLIGENCE SUMMARY

Army Form C. 2118

Hour, Date, Place	Summary of Events and Information	Remarks and references to Appendices
Trenches R3-Q7 3rd June 1915 9.30 a.m.	Officers of 2nd Gurkhas went down with a view to relief	Casualties - 3 wounded by rifle fire
10 a.m.	Brigadier visited trenches.	
	Hostile aircraft active during day. Hostile artillery less active. Machine gun relieved our machine gun.	
9 p.m.	Left Gun of Right Gun of 4th Gurkhas relieved Left Gun of Right Gun of 2nd Gurkhas	
9.30 p.m. 11.30 p.m.	Relief of Battn commenced. Relief completed and Battn. relieved by Coys. to Billets in King George Road — One Coy. being Bde Reserve.	2 Reinforcements and 4 sick reports from Marseilles
King George Road 4th June 1915	Battn at rest in Billets. Baggage waggons brought up.	
5th June 1915	Battn in Billets	Casualties
6th June 1915	Battn in Billets	1 Man wounded Rifle Fire
7th June 1915 3 p.m.	Brigade Relieved by GARHWAL BDE. Battn. relieved by 2/8th Gurkha Rifles and marched by Portion of 2 Platoons to Billets round from Road R28d VIEILLE CHAPELLE via LA COUTURE	
4.30 p.m.	Battn. completed move into new Billets	

WAR DIARY
INTELLIGENCE SUMMARY

Army Form C. 2118.

Hour, Date, Place	Summary of Events and Information	Remarks and references to Appendices
Billets, VIEILLE CHAPELLE 8th June 1915	Right Half Batt: now one of baths in Brewery VIEILLE CHAPELLE.	2nd Lt DOWE (interpreter) left to rejoin Army War Office. Lieut: F. Abery proceeded to England on 7 days leave.
9th June 1915.	Left Half Batt: Aso one of Baths in Brewery. No 2789 L/t TIKARAM KANWAR awarded 2nd Class IOM by the Comr in Chief for gallantry in bringing in L/Corpl Gregory 1st Bn from between the British and German trenches on 26th May 1915.	3 Wounded [Sick] reported from 1st R.
10th June 1915	Parades under Coy Comd'rs otherwise slack.	§ 1 wounded § Reinforcement from middle
11th June 1915	Major Nicholson 17.S. relieving Capt Gubbay 17.S. from medical charge of the Batt.	
2.45 p.m.	The Brigade inspected by Lieut Gen Sir James Willcock Comm Indian Corps.	
12th June 1915	2 Parades daily (Sunday excepted) unless by Comm =	(12th) 3 Sick reported 1st R
13th	Lieut: Puran Singh Khokha and 60 Reinforcements from 1st R = 22	his 10 yrs with Jullah Extg party returns to India.
14th	Batt: joined from India (13.6.15)	(16th) 2 wounded & 1 Sick from 1st R
15th		(16th) L. Bevery returns from leave Capt Pyke proceeded on 8 days leave
16th		

WAR DIARY
or
INTELLIGENCE SUMMARY. 76

(Erase heading not required.)

Army Form C. 2118.

Hour, Date, Place	Summary of Events and Information	Remarks and references to Appendices
VIEILLE CHAPELLE 17th June 1915	Battn. continuing with Brigade relief of Bareilly Bde. moved by Peloton to relieve 69th Punjabis in Kings Road. (X 11 d 76 South westwards to X 11 c 10/6)	
6.30 p.m.	Relief completed. Battn. in Brigade Reserve	
18th June 1915 8 a.m.	Fatigue of 112 C.O. and 75 men to unload carts at Junction Kings Road and King George Road	
19th June 1915 Noon	Brigadier visits Battn.	
7.30 a.m.	Officers Cos. by Coys. and Adjt. went Subsection A	
9 a.m.	M.G. detachment went up to relieve M.Gs. husband Guns in Subsection "A"	
9.15 a.m.	Working Party of 1 25o men under Capt [?] and Capt Arrowsmith to obtain Coy's [?] from Right of Reserve to Support in Subsection A	2 Sikh Regiment from I.F.A.
20th June	Fatigue of 1 12 C.O. and 15 men to unload carts as per	
10 [?]		
7 a.m. 21st June	Guides Officer visit Subsection A Brigadier visits Battn. H.Qs	1 Sikh Regiment from I.F.A.

Army Form C. 2118.

WAR DIARY
or
INTELLIGENCE SUMMARY.

(Erase heading not required.)

77

Hour, Date, Place	Summary of Events and Information	Remarks and references to Appendices
Kemp Road 6 pm 21st June 1915 2/30 am	Signallers go round Telephone system of new trenches	
	Dressing stations at Brigadier [Lieut Col] Witchcombe Dugout	
22nd June 1915 10 am	Capt Amworth rode as member of Field General Court martial on 2 men of 10th Regulars Hrs.	
11 am	Brigadier visits Batt. H.Q.	
23rd June 1915 6.30 pm 9.30 pm	Signallers go up to take over the line Relief of A Subsection 6" Jets commenced. Parties wounded from J.Os by trench alongside from being out to ammunition intense, raking gunfire on Rue du Bois.	2nd Lt Arth[..] from Batt'n for 1 A R posted to No 2 Cy 2 wounded T 15 fetch up Pte[..] Lt Col Witchcombe wounded in [..] dugout & [..] Casualties 1 wounded
24 June 1915	Relief completed 6" Jets withdrawn to Kemp Road took carried out to adjust the Gaps to no responsible disposition. They are 6 Platoons { No. Right to 2 Cy { on Left to 3 Cy Supports 6 Platoon (No 4 Cy and 1 Platoon No 2 Cy) Reserve No 1 Cy 4 Machine Guns in line (2 Regt and 2, 6" Jets Guns) Bomb Prooft and Splinter Proofs Built in Parados of the trench Old German Com Trench T.P.11 Masses by fatigue squad 105 Battn RFA Gave us [..] trench	Lt Col G.J. Witchcombe admitted to companion of the Bath

WAR DIARY
or
INTELLIGENCE SUMMARY.

(Erase heading not required.)

Army Form C. 2118.

Hour, Date, Place	Summary of Events and Information	Remarks and references to Appendices
Sub Section "A" RDE DE BOIS. 25th June 1915		
Before Dawn	Grass cut to 20 yds in front of wire before daylight. Communication Trenches deepened and Parados splinter Proofs in	Casualties 1 Killed 1 Wounded
	The French continued Patrols reported enemy working in their trenches and chimney in Foya	1 Sick man reported from 1F.A.
4 pm - 5 pm	Communication Trenches and Fire Trenches Rifle-Grenaded	
26th June 1915	44th Batty R.F.A. Relieved 205 Batty R.F.A. covering our front. Patrols encounter German Patrol or men killed. Capt Gore went out to see if N.C.O. on report was correct and was killed. His body was recovered. Little Rifle fire or our Parapet.	Casualties 5 wounded 2 Killed Capt Gore - Killed
11 am	Hun and Com: Trenches Rifle-Grenaded.	
4 pm	Support shelled by Howitzer.	
27 June 1915 6.10 pm	Settling commenced. Enemy Working Parts dispersed by our 2 G. Rifles in their Piquet Post on QUINQUE RUE	Casualties 1 Wounded
11 am	Germans reported working in their Piquet Post by front water.	
28th June 1915 Before Dawn	Advanced trench joined up and deepened to 3 ft. Com. Piquet Post to centre of Piquet St Leta.	Casualties 1 Killed
11 am	Prowse Road shelled by heavier shells HE and Com. Trenches Piquet preparation during day.	

Army Form C. 2118.

WAR DIARY
or
INTELLIGENCE SUMMARY. Z9
(Erase heading not required.)

Instructions regarding War Diaries and Intelligence Summaries are contained in F. S. Regs., Part II. and the Staff Manual respectively. Title pages will be prepared in manuscript.

Hour, Date, Place	Summary of Events and Information	Remarks and references to Appendices
PRINCESS ROAD, Richebourg 29th June	Wire put up in front of Support Trench, and general improvements carried out on line	Casualties 1. Wounded
11 am 4 pm	Artillery fire. Enemy's artillery & ours active "SNIPER" activities of snipers in Support trench must be put down by day and fire directed onto German trenches.	
10.30 pm	Trench and fire trench have been put in readiness for relief but carrying on connection work	
30th June 1.30 am	1st Coy of 4th Seaforths arrive to commence relief. Relief completed. Companies arrive in billets in Kings Road promptly exposed by Battn: Battn: M.G. Detachment relieved by 4th Seaforths.	Casualties 1. Wounded

G.V. Hillicombe Lt Col
Comg 1/5 G R

Serial No. 96.

121/6502

WAR DIARY
OF
1/9th Gurkha Rifles.

FROM 1st July 1915 TO 31st July 1915

Army Form C. 2118.

WAR DIARY
or
INTELLIGENCE SUMMARY.
(Erase heading not required.)

80

Instructions regarding War Diaries and Intelligence Summaries are contained in F. S. Regs., Part II. and the Staff Manual respectively. Title pages will be prepared in manuscript.

Hour, Date, Place	Summary of Events and Information	Remarks and references to Appendices
KING'S ROAD 1st July 1915 6 am	Battn remained in Billets in Constant Readiness	
8.30 pm	Fatigue of 1 N.C.O and 20 men to trench Telephone Wire	Whole
9.30 pm	2 Lt Duncan & 200 men on fatigue in "C" Subsection	
	1 N.C.O and 15 men industry work under Capt Firth	
2nd July 1915 8 am	Fatigue of 1 N.C.O & 20 men hanging Telephone wires	
8.30 pm	2 Lt Dobbs and 200 men on fatigue in "C" Subsection	
6.30 pm	C.O. by Cmn & Adjt went to "C" Subsection	1 Wounded Regimtl
3rd July 9.30 am	1 N.C.O & 18 men hanging Telephone wires	
8.30 pm	Relief of 6th Batt in "C" Subsection commenced by Battn	
midnight	Relief completed without incident	
H.Q "C" Subsection RUE DE BOIS		
	Firing Line Right No I Coy (Capt Pike)	
	Left No IV Coy (Capt Hardman)	
	2 Battn Machine Guns - 2 Guns 107th Pioneers - 1 Gun 4th Cavalry	
	Supports No III Coy (Capt Ainsworth)	
	Reserve No II Coy (West Riydrs)	
	H.Q. RUE DE BOIS	

WAR DIARY or INTELLIGENCE SUMMARY.

Army Form C. 2118

81

(Erase heading not required.)

Hour, Date, Place	Summary of Events and Information	Remarks and references to Appendices
RUE DU BOIS C Sector 4th July 1915. 7 pm	Hostile aeroplane came over our line and again after daybreak when no fire was offered with Rennie. Trenches were cleaned up, and fire stops adjusted to Gontchev Requirements.	
7 pm	Hostile aeroplane again came over our line but were driven back by fire of our Anti-aircraft guns.	
5th July 1915	During early hours before daylight CADBURY Comms. Trench was improved - Bayonet trench into the French Paradox & inspection trench were improved.	2 Sick reported from 1st R
4.30 am	Hostile Aeroplane in spite of the fire of our anti-aircraft guns crossed our lines flying high N.W.	
2 am	Patrol heard carts being unloaded near Q12 - Q14 and a motor lorry near that point.	
9.30 pm	Shelling tube tunnel due probably to large working party of 150 men 6 Iota continued work on new Support trench.	
6th July 1915. 5 am	Hostile aeroplane again over our line at 5 am when our aircraft gun opened fire. Shelling was above usual experienced especially on Support Trench T Q2 - Q3	Casualties Wounded 5

Forms/C. 2118/10

Army Form C. 2118

WAR DIARY
or
INTELLIGENCE SUMMARY.
(Erase heading not required.)

82

Hour, Date, Place	Summary of Events and Information	Remarks and references to Appendices
RUE DU BOIS "C" Schuster 6th July 1915	Patrols reported that Hand Grenade Posts were indicated between our O.12-11-14 patrols owing to fire in trenches. Walk Colthorp On Trench from support to the trench completed. The Shuster trench behind Farm Corner was converted into a fire trench.	
7th July 1915 5 a.m.	Hostile Aeroplane flying N.W. very high (over) our lines at 5 a.m.	Lt. Poynor goes on 7 days leave
12.30 a.m.	Shelling rather normal. Our Guns — 14th Battn R.F.A. covering us, just stopped a German working party by their fire. General improvements were carried out in the line.	
11 a.m.	Col Widdrinton left Staff to assume command of the Sehra Dun Brigade vice General Twich on leave.	Capt Ainsworth goes on 7 days leave
6.30 p.m.	Capt Markman assumes command Relief of Battn: by 6th Jats commenced	Lt Kenway goes to Rattam Refreshes No G. Course at MOLINGHEM
11.15 p.m.	Relief completed	
midnight	Battn in billets in KING GEORGES ROAD	
8th July 1915 KING GEORGES ROAD 6.30 p.m.	Battn: rest in billets. Fatigue of 1 G.O. + 30 men carrying material to 6th Jats Fatigue of 1 G.O. + 50 men to work in C Schuster	

Army Form C. 2118.

WAR DIARY
or
INTELLIGENCE SUMMARY.
(Erase heading not required.)

83

Instructions regarding War Diaries and Intelligence Summaries are contained in F.S. Regs., Part II. and the Staff Manual respectively. Title pages will be prepared in manuscript.

Hour, Date, Place	Summary of Events and Information	Remarks and references to Appendices
KING GEORGES ROAD 9th July 1915	Batt'n in Billets. Fatigues to clean up Billets	Lieut Taylor transferred to 6/35 G.R. 3 wounded rejoin 9/14 Sick +1 Reinforcement
10th July 1915 8 pm	Batt'n moved off en route for new Billets near St FLORIS. In rent Brigade relieved by 21st Bde	
8.45 pm	Batt'n clear of RICHEBOURG.	
11th July 1915	Batt'n arrived in new Billets	
St FLORIS 12th July 1915	— L'EPINETTE — CALONNE. Parades time checks at 10.10 am and in afternoon Rifle Exercises etc	1 wounded + 1 Sick rejoined 2nd Lt Duncan goes on 7 days leave
13th July 1915 10 am	Route hand under C.O. through St FLORIS + St VENANT. M. ROBIDNY french Interpreter (Sergeant of 114th Reg't) awarded the CROIX DE GUERRE and mentioned in French orders du Jour Général No 28 of the French Mission attached to the B.E.F.	1 Sick rejoined from I.F.A. 1 Bn + 1 B been transferred to MERVILLE
14th July 1915	Parades morning + evening under Coy Comrs.	Lieut Murray proceeded on leave Lieut Paynter returned from leave
15th July 1915	Comp'y Parades, and Bomb Battery Gun offices L' Gen Sir James Willcocks visits the Men.	

Army Form C. 2118.

WAR DIARY
or
INTELLIGENCE SUMMARY.
(Erase heading not required.)

84

Instructions regarding War Diaries and Intelligence Summaries are contained in F. S. Regs., Part II. and the Staff Manual respectively. Title pages will be prepared in manuscript.

Hour, Date, Place	Summary of Events and Information	Remarks and references to Appendices
St FLORIS 10 a.m. 16th July 1915	Route march under C.O.	
9 p.m.	Cinema show for Batt- men behind stables	
17th July 1915	Morning & afternoon parades under Coy Comdrs. Inter Three match with Bde Signal Coys. Score 5-4	1 Sub. howr. gun arrived from I.F.A. Capt Ainsworth appointed from Divn. 1st Kings gave 6 M.G. course. 4 Pack reymds from I.F.A.
18th July 1915	Batt- rests in billets. (Sunday) Muster Parade at 11 am	
19th July 1915	Coys Parades	Newitch rides at 9 p.m.
20th July 1915	Bomb Throwing Practice. Bomb accident in No 3 Coy. 2 men died of wounds & 2 men slightly wounded.	Capt Shackleton goes on 7 days leave
11 am	Lieut Craft unit Inst Dobbs Inst Paine bey Khoilil inspected near MERVILLE by G.O.C. Indian Corps	Lieut Murray wears his Majestys the King's add Winston Castle and afterwards lunches at the Castle
6 p.m.	Inter Three match v. 8th Battn R.F.A. Won 5-2	MILITARY CROSS from his
21st July 1915 10 am	Cont of Engrs way into Bomb accident	
1 p.m.	No 1 Coy were Divn Baths at CALONNE.	
10 am	Batt- team No 1 Coy for Route march.	
9 am	Lieut Pryor & Representatives to Bomb display to No 3 Coy S-M. at VERT BOIS	
22nd July 1915 4.30 pm	Company Parades. Lieut Spurkley Sub. Bhindu Khittri & 69 men join from 2nd base as reinforcement. Marseilles	Inter-three match will beyond Coy Wm S-m L

WAR DIARY or INTELLIGENCE SUMMARY

Army Form C. 2118
85

Hour, Date, Place	Summary of Events and Information	Remarks and references to Appendices
ST FLORIS. 23rd July 1915	Coys Parade.	1 Man reported (B Coy) from Reserve
2 pm	Football match against Signal Coy, won 3-2.	
3 pm	Photographer visited Battn and took photos & cinema	
4.30 pm	film of Football tournament began (1st Round)	"A" beat F & C beat A
24th July 1915	Inter Coy Football tournament continues, 1st Round	"B" beat G & D beat E
25th July 1915	Company Parades.	Lt. Col. WIDDICOMBE returned to C.B. from the Majesty The King
	Company Tournament. Semi- Final Round	at WINDSOR CASTLE and Dinner
	"C" beat H Coy & "B" beat D Coy	at the CASTLE.
26th July 1915	Company parades	
	Final of Company Tournament "B" Coy beat C Coy 1-0	
27th July 1915	Col Widdicombe returned from leave	
	10 a.m. B & B× been inspected by L.G. Comd Manchester	
	at Bde H.Qs. ST FLORIS	
12.40 pm	Lost Regiment under Lieut Spackley inspected by	Footh Whitworth 8" howr
	L.G.C near MERVILLE	R.F.A how 2-1
3 pm	Battn to Bde Gymkhana	M.J Rotherry (Interpreter)
28th July 1915	Brigade Gymkhana begins Hales boxing tourney in	transferred to ???
10.30	Evening in 2d G.R. Billets	
	Battn. Billets and in Evening in 2d G.R. Billets	

Army Form C. 2118.

WAR DIARY
or
INTELLIGENCE SUMMARY.
(Erase heading not required.)

86

Hour, Date, Place	Summary of Events and Information	Remarks and references to Appendices
ST FLORIS 29th July 1915	Batt: won following Prizes in Home Shirt Gymkhana. 1st Line Transport Turn out — 1st Prize. Machine Gun detachment — 1st Prize. Transport Horses (Pairs) — 1st & 2nd Prizes. Slinging of 3 Transport Mules — 2nd Prize.	
29th July 1915 10.30 am	Parades under Company Comdrs. C.O inspects Cat: onwards	1 Sick regrn from I.F.A
30th July 1915 7 am	1 Wounded and 20 Sick regrns from Havrincourt Route Marches under Comp: Officers to HAVERSKIRK	Another batch with 2nd Batt R.F.A men 2 - 1
2.30 pm 6.30 pm	Capt Mackinnon regrns from leave B Battery R.F.A. Sports. C.O & Adjt: attend conference at Bde Hdqrs	
31st July 1915	Comp Comdrs Hd1s inspection parades, and Ammunion inspect rifles of Batt:	
10.30 am	Lt Payne-Beverly officer visits new Billeting area at LA GORGUE	

G.H. Williamson Lt Col
Comdg 1/9th Gurkha Rifles

Serial No. 96

12/6948

WAR DIARY
OF
1st Battalion 9th Gurkha Rifles.

FROM 1st August 1915 To 31st August 1915

Army Form C. 2118.

WAR DIARY
or
INTELLIGENCE SUMMARY.
(Erase heading not required.)

Instructions regarding War Diaries and Intelligence Summaries are contained in F.S. Regs., Part II. and the Staff Manual respectively. Title pages will be prepared in manuscript.

Hour, Date, Place	Summary of Events and Information	Remarks and references to Appendices
1st August 1915 ST FLORIS. 10.15 a.m.	The Battⁿ marched to new Billets at LA GORGUE and reached new Billeting Area Sq R12a.	1st Sick report from Battⁿ [illegible]. Major Mackelvie goes on 7 days leave. Lieut Pethun (Interpreter) joins Battⁿ.
2nd August 1915 LA GORGUE 10 am	Medical inspection of men who fell out. Route march for men who fell out under 2/Lieut Botha	
3 pm	I.G.O. (Genl Baba Bartolomeo Whistler and 56 men of 12th Battⁿ) for Battⁿ for Rounders. Reinforcements from Regt in front line attached to Battⁿs	
3rd August 1915 10.30 am	Route march for men who fell out under 2nd Battⁿs. Parades for remainder of Battⁿ under C.O. inspects new Reinforcement. Company Parades.	3 men rejoined from I.F.A. L. Murray joins Battⁿ on Brigade Grenadier officer. 6 men (w.f.t.) sent off.
4th August 1915 7 pm	Digging fatigue of 400 men under Capt Pike to improve new Reserve Trench near RUE TILLELOY	2 (C.M.) to Menunce 4 (Sick) to Dus Aux Cul. 1 man rejoins from I.F.A.
5th August 1915	Parades with Company arrangements.	
6th August 1915 12 noon	Company Parades. 2/Lieut French & 24 men go to LINGHEM to test M.guns. Telescopic Rifles etc [illegible]	7 Captⁿ & to Sheerut Salvage coy. L. Kempt goes on 7 days leave.

WAR DIARY
or
INTELLIGENCE SUMMARY.

Army Form C. 2118.

88

(Erase heading not required.)

Hour, Date, Place	Summary of Events and Information	Remarks and references to Appendices
LA GORGUE 6: Aug 5.15 p.m.	Polo match with Royal Artillery at Estaires. Lose 2 Chukkars 3-0. Lieuts Barry, Spratley, Murray, & Poynder play.	
7: Aug 1915 10 a.m.	C.O. & Adjt try again to visit "B" Subsection & go round trenches held by 2d Leicesters with a view to relieving that Regt.	M.G. detachment went into line. 1 man rejoined from 1/5 A
8: Aug 1915 7.40 p.m.	Battn moved to relieve 2d Leicesters in B Subsection moving by Coys at 10 min intervals via PONT DU HEM and RUGBY ROAD.	Capt Pike goes sick Draft: Runners Smg returns to India 4: Bothan transferred to W.3
11. p.m.	Relief Completed.	
9: Aug 1915 11 a.m.	A quiet day. 5 p.m. g.r. Knowards point 197. The Brigadier visited HQrs. Disposition in B Subsection Firing line & Supports. Nos 1 - 3 & 4 Coys. Reserve No 2 Coy with 1 Platoon in TILLELOY South Fort M.G. 2 Guns Battr & 1 Gun 4: Seaforth in line	Casualties 1 killed 1 man rejoined from 1/5A
10: Aug 1915	Work of improvement of the line carried out. Brigadier & L.G. visit go round line. Capt Hannah & Lt Sandford, 4: Cavalry attached to Battn for instruction	

WAR DIARY
or
INTELLIGENCE SUMMARY.
(Erase heading not required.)

Army Form C. 2118.

89

Hour, Date, Place	Summary of Events and Information	Remarks and references to Appendices
B Sector RUE TILLELOY 11th Aug 1915 2 pm	General improvement of the line continued. A quiet day, little sniper or artillery fire. Lt Col G.T. Woolcombe C.B. goes to BQ in Sergt "Evans" Car. Capt A.C.B. Buckingham assumes command.	Casualties 1 killed 1 man reported to 1st FA
4 pm	Bund 7 Practices Red Rocket.	
12th Aug 1915	Work of improving Existing Cmt: Trenches & making strong dugouts in the back continued	Shell Red 3/4 in by about 15 where shells Casualties 2 wounded
6 am	Hostile Minenwerfer put over 11 shells (no flame) from Pt 197 without causing damage	
11 am	C.O. + Adjt 1st Seaforth 44th Visit Stns to arrange reliefs	
6 pm	Coy Cmdrs visit Sectors to see line	
10.30 pm	Relief commenced	
13th Aug 1915 1 am 2 am	Relief completed.	
8 pm	Battn arrived in Billets PONT DU HEM in B. Reserve. 4 Drummer + 200 men a digging fatigue to in support line under orders of Capt Stanley Clarke (Intelligence officer) until 1am. Found stores or carrying work 30 men under orders of 2nd Lt Smith	Capt Harman JY Seaforths Reported to Commander on arrival here next

Army Form C. 2118.

WAR DIARY
or
INTELLIGENCE SUMMARY.
(Erase heading not required.)

Instructions regarding War Diaries and Intelligence Summaries are contained in F.S. Regs., Part II. and the Staff Manual respectively. Title pages will be prepared in manuscript.

Hour, Date, Place	Summary of Events and Information	Remarks and references to Appendices
PONT DU HEM		
14th Aug 1915	2/Lt Burke J.A.R. joined the Battⁿ	
8.45 pm	Lt Spurling & 1350 men on Digging Fatigue under Capt Shawphin in new Support line.	Casualties 1 man killed.
8.50 pm	Capt Ainsworth, 2/Lt Finch & 250 men on Carrying Fatigue to 3rd S.Tr	3 men Reprs for I.F.A 1 Vicker Bomber arrives.
15th Aug 1915	Company Fatigue to 3rd S.Tr under Lieut Kemp 6/10 in^g	Lieut Kemp rejoins from leave.
9 pm		Takes over 2 M.Gs 6" Tels
16th Aug 1915	C.O. Adj^t and Company Com^{rs} visit "A" Subsection with a view to relieving 2nd Gorkhas & 1 coy 1st Seaforths.	
10 am	No 3 Coy moves from Rifleto to commence relief	
8.50 pm	Followed at intervals of 10 min by Companies via Rouge Croix & Sign Post Lane.	
12 mn	Relief complete	
17th Aug 1915	Disposition (Right Sup Post Lane Inclusive to Colon Gou'wal Inclusive)	
	Firing line { No 1 Coy Lt Prior; No 2 Coy Lt Shreeve	
	Supports { No 2 Coy Capt Ainsworth & 2 Platoons No 4 Coy No 3 Coy in his vicinity, 1 Vicker in Sup Post	
	Reserve in "B" line, 2 Platoons No 4 Coy	Casualties – Nil
	H.Q. Ebenezer Farm in Rue Tilleloy Quiet day little Rifle or Shell fire avoided at intervals	

WAR DIARY or INTELLIGENCE SUMMARY.

(Erase heading not required.)

Army Form C. 2118.

Hour, Date, Place	Summary of Events and Information	Remarks and references to Appendices
EBENEZER FARM H.Qrs "A" Subsector 18th Aug 1915		
10 am	Col Widdicombe assumes Command of the Battn=	
noon	The Brigadier visits the line	
	Quiet day. Situation normal.	
8.30 pm	Bombing Parties occupied Ruined House at Post 143	Casualties - 1 Wounded
19th Aug 1915	Situation normal	
8.30 pm	Machine Gun fire opened on Roads and Approaches behind German line	Casualties - 1 Wounded
	Desultory rifle Battn= in "A" Subsector front covered by Rfl 2nd & 7th Battys R.F.A.	
20th Aug 1915	During morning offensive 2nd Gorkhas Rifle line with a view to relief	Casualties - 2 Wounded
	2 white Bulls. Sgts= Baghu Rana & 7 O.R.'s of Pltns transferred to 1/4th Gurkha Rifles to proceed to Marseilles and Beyrut.	
8.30 pm		
9 pm	Relief of "A" Subsector commenced by 2nd G.R.	
11.30 pm	Relief Completed	Machine guns returned at 6 pm. 1 M.G. left in line. 1 Vickers left in Lafone Post.
	20 H Boys under 2/Lt Swinnan remain in "B" line in Reserve.	
	No. 1 Coy Trench.... I.G.D. (Set= Bethlehem Thapa) 40 men ..... "B" LAFONE POST	

Army Form C. 2118.

WAR DIARY
or
INTELLIGENCE SUMMARY.
(Erase heading not required.)

92

Hour, Date, Place	Summary of Events and Information	Remarks and references to Appendices
Port du Hem 8.145 21st June 1915 Night	Working Party of 250 men under Capt Blackburn & 2nd Lt Burke under a Capt Sheringham. To work on new Communication Trench	1 wounded rejoined from 1FA.
22nd June 1915. 8.30 pm	Carrying party of 250 men under Lieuts Shuckley & Finch to carry up frames from RUE DE BACQUEROT to "B" Lines	
23rd June 1915 8.45 pm 8.40 pm	Digging Party under Capt Ainsworth of 150 men. Digging Party of 80 men under Lieut Kemp. Both under instruction of Capt Sheringham to work on Communication Trenches.	No English Mail
7 pm	Remaining Machine Guns of Battn came out of the line	
24th June 1915 7 pm Evening	Took over garrison duty of undermentioned posts – MIN Post – Jem. Labhsham + 25 men (2o. Coy) RUGBY Post – Jem. Saunderson + 25 men (No. 2 Coy) ROUGE CROIX EAST – Jem. Whiteman + 38 men (No 3 Coy)	1 Sick 1 Wounded } Rejoined from 1FA 1 man wounded
8.45 pm Midnight	Battn moved by Companies to Billets near LAGORGUE. 2nd & 3rd Coy to one Platoon & 1 by regular route.	
25th June 1915	Battn – Rest in Billets Battn Polo match v Cheshires in afternoon. 1st Innings Shuckley Poynter & Kemp Play. v 13th Cavalry Lost 3–2	

Army Form C. 2118.

WAR DIARY
or
INTELLIGENCE SUMMARY.
(Erase heading not required.)

93

Hour, Date, Place	Summary of Events and Information	Remarks and references to Appendices
LA GORGUE 26 Aug /15	Batt⁰ has one of Batt⁰ⁿˢ at LESTREM and PONT RIQUEUL the whole Batt⁰ⁿˢ toilin.	
8.15 pm	Working parts to build new tram way to RUE BACQUEROT of 100 men under 2/L Duncan	
5 pm	Details of various Reg⁺ˢ arrive and are attached to Batt⁰ⁿˢ for 8 days.	4 Rifle 6 numerous} reports to Boulogne
	Capt Mackenna } + 162} Officers Jn 58ᵗʰ Rifles + 4/c Dunford }	
	2/8ᵗʰ G⁺R 1 G.O & 10 O.R.I. 2/3ʳᵈ G⁺R 8 O.R.I. 39ᵗʰ Garhwalis 7 O.R.I. 107ᵗʰ Pioneers 30 O.R.I (Jo 107ˢ Pioneers) Last 35ᵗʰ Signal Coy 11 O.R.I.	
27ᵗʰ Aug/15 10am	C.O. + Adj⁺ go to staff Ride near Robeck with G.O.C. Batt⁰ moves to new Billets in Square L.26.(Sheet 36)	Casualties - nil
11am		
8.30 pm	Working party at Rue Bacquerot of 400 men under Capt Mackenna + 2/Lt Burke	
8 pm	Working party from men in Parts of about 100 men under Lieut Spackly on trucking tram line	

WAR DIARY
or
INTELLIGENCE SUMMARY.

Army Form C. 2118.

94

(Erase heading not required.)

Hour, Date, Place	Summary of Events and Information	Remarks and references to Appendices
Squares L26 28th Aug 1915 5 p.m.	Return to Post. Mar, Rugby & Rouge Croix East move under Adjutant	
8.30 p.m.	Relief Completed	
11 p.m.	Relieved Party arrives in Billets	
5 p.m.	Football match v Royal Flying Corps Win 1 – 0	
29th Aug 1915 10 a.m.	Details attached to "Batt" were to join their Depôts	
5.30 p.m.	Batt moved into new Billets at Rugby Road. Arriving in Transport at 7.30 p.m. Remaining in its Billets. 1st Line Transport under Lieut Duncan.	Lieut Berry proceeds on 7 days leave
6.30 p.m.	Working Party 200 men Capt Mellis on new Communication Trench near Rue Capt. Hindesworth	
8.30 p.m.	Carrying Party 200 men	
Rugby Road 30th Aug 1915 9 p.m.	Carrying Party of 300 men under Lieut Keyte & Lieut Burke, to carry material to "B" Line from Rue Bacquerot	2 sick rejoined from I.F.A. 1 wounded transfd to I.F.A.
31st Aug 1915 8 p.m.	Carrying Party of "C" & "D" 400 men under Captain Thackthorn Lieut Spreckly carrying material to "B", "D" Line from Rue Bacquerot.	2 sick rejoined from I.F.A.

G. Williams
LIEUT. COLONEL
Commanding 1st. Bn. 9th. Gurkha Rifles.

Serial No. 96.

121/7286

WAR DIARY
OF
1st Battalion 9th Gurkha Rifles.

From 1st September 1915 To 30th September 1915

WAR DIARY or INTELLIGENCE SUMMARY.

(Erase heading not required.)

Army Form C. 2118.

95

Hour, Date, Place	Summary of Events and Information	Remarks and references to Appendices
RUGBY ROAD.		
September 1st 1915. 7.30 p.m.	Working party 100 men under Lieut Duncan to bury telephone wires from Rue Bacquerot to firing line.	
	Carrying party of 180 men under Captain Ridsworth to carry material from EUSTON POST to firing line.	
Sept. 2nd 1915. 7.30 p.m.	Working party 100 men under Lieut Burke burying telephone wires near Rue Tilleloy.	4 sick rep'd from I.F.A.
8 p.m.	Working party 200 men under Lieut Kemp digging communication trench between Rue Bacquerot & B line.	Sgt. GOPINATH AGGARWAL joined the Bn.
2 p.m.	ROUGE CROIX EAST, RUGBY and MAIN POSTS relieved by Garhwal Bde.	
3.30 p.m.	Batt. O.P. machine guns go into huts in M.S.B.	2 sick
Sept. 3rd 1915. 7 p.m.	50 men under Subr. Puran Sing Khandka carrying party.	1 Regr. from I.F.A. 1 Wounded
7.30 p.m.	Working party of 100 men under Lieut Spackley on Com. Trench.	

Army Form C. 2118

WAR DIARY
or
INTELLIGENCE SUMMARY.
(Erase heading not required.)

Hour, Date, Place	Summary of Events and Information	Remarks and references to Appendices
RUG-BY ROAD 10 AM 4th Sept 1915	Officers visit trenches IND'S. B with a view to taking over from 69th Punjabis	3 Sick reported from 1st A
8.40 pm	Batt: moved into line to relieve 69th Punjabis. Disposition. Firing Line 6 machine Guns 1 Batt: {No 2 Coy Lieut Spackley / No 3 Coy Capt Ellsworth / No 4 Coy Capt Markman with 1 Platoon No 1 Coy} Supports {No 1 Coy Lieut Burke less 1 Platoon / North 1 coy 1st Rajputs} Reserve B. line. Remainder 1st Rajputs Hd. Qrs. at Cockbet House	
Cockbet House 5th Sept 1915 10 pm	Quiet day both of infirmary dugouts carried out. Lieut Spackley and Lieut Brokenshaw Maratha wounded by bomb while reconnoitring up ditch towards German trench. Lieut Knup taken change of no 2.	4 men wounded
6th Sept 1915	Quiet day, work continued on improving dugouts	1st Sikh Reynor fm 2 wounded Marseilles

WAR DIARY
INTELLIGENCE SUMMARY
(Erase heading not required.)

Army Form C. 2118

Hour, Date, Place	Summary of Events and Information	Remarks and references to Appendices
CUTHBERT HOUSE IND S. B. 7th Sept. 1915	Lieut Col G.T. Widdicombe C.B. takes over temporary command of 1. S. D. Bde.	Lieut Ramsey reports from leave Casualties - 1 wounded 3 sick reports from I.S.B.
8 pm	Capt. ac B. Hutchison takes command of the Batt= Reinforcement of 61 O.R.1 from Invaliders Lieut Popham taken over No 2 Coy	
8th Sept 1915	Batt= relieved in Front Line by 1st Seaforths and withdrawn to "B" Lines. No 1. Coy under Lieut Burke moves into him Post and Rue de Bacquerot	Casualties - 2 wounded 1 Sick reports from I.S.B.
5 pm		
10.30 pm	Fatigue of 200 men under Lieut Burke to dig from R. Lieut Popham to continue	
9th Sept 1915	Fatigue of 100 men under Lieut Popham continues	
9 pm	from Start	
9 pm	No men under Sgt. Blundell to Duke's Rd.	
9 pm	South of road Jewelry Start	
10th Sept 1915	100 men under Capt Ainsworth on Carrying fatigue from Cuthbert House to Duke's Rd	
10 am	Lieut Duncan and 60 men on Fatigue in Duke's Bill	
9.30 pm	Parties at work by day on improving Rue Report	
11th Sept 1915	Circle Rue du Bacquerot, and cleaning up Wellesley Start Trench Start, and Wellesley Start	
9.30 pm	100 men under Lieut Burke at work on Duke's Rd.	

WAR DIARY
or
INTELLIGENCE SUMMARY.
(Erase heading not required.)

Army Form C. 2118

Hour, Date, Place	Summary of Events and Information	Remarks and references to Appendices
CONDUIT STREET IND 5.B 12th Sept 1915	Parties at work as in 11th on cleaning up Communication trenches.	
	33 men carry amm. from Horie Counties Trench to 'B' Lines	
5.30 pm	Battn commences withdrawal by Pelotons to Billets via La Gorgue via rue Street - LA FLINQUE - LE DRUMEZ and from there a a Battn via Estaires	
10 pm	Battn arrives in new Billets (Sheet 36a A 27 E.) Machine Guns also withdrawn from line	
13th Sept 1915	men Battn try parties in Command	
14th Sept 1915 1 p.m.	Right Half Battn Remainder of Battn were baths at PONT RICQUEUL	Lieut Col Widdicombe rejoins Battn & took over Com?
5.30 pm.	Carrying Party of 300 men under Capt Ainsworth & Lieut Kempt taken in carts to RUGBY ROAD to carry material to 'R' lines	
15th Sept 1915	Left Half Battn use Baths at PONT RICQUEUL. Remainder under Comp? Com?	
16th Sept 1915 8 am	Remainder under Comp? Com?	Capt Pile rejoins from Sick leave

WAR DIARY or INTELLIGENCE SUMMARY

Army Form C. 2118.

99

Hour, Date, Place	Summary of Events and Information	Remarks and references to Appendices
LA GORGUE. 4.7.f. 17th Sept 1915. 10.a.m. 9.a.m.	C.O. and Adjutant visit H.Q. IND.S.f. Capt Parsons and 40 men Jm Batts from Marseilles an Reinforcement. New Brigade Comr visits H.Qrs and meets British & Gurkha officers Passes under Company Comrs	
18th Sept 1915. 4.45 p.m. 9.30 p.m.	The Batt- moved to take over hd & R from composite Batt- of Bareilly Brigade under Lt Ridgeway 33rd Punjabis via ESTAIRES - LA BASSEE Road and RUGBY Road Left Half Batt- via BIRDCAGE STREET Right Half Batt- via N TILLELOY STREET Relief completed Batt- H.Q. and Supportes took over line at midday Disposition Firing Line & Supports South Trenches Grenage to both Tilleloys - No I Coy - Lt Poynder both Tilleloy to train St. - No II Coy - Capt Parsons train St. to Birdcage St. - No III Coy - Capt Ainsworth. Birdcage to Winchester Road. - No IV Coy - Capt Lutman Reserve 1st Support line in "B" line. H.Qrs - Arthur House	

WAR DIARY
or
INTELLIGENCE SUMMARY

Army Form C. 2118.

Hour, Date, Place	Summary of Events and Information	Remarks and references to Appendices
CUTHBERT HOUSE IND 5. B. 19th to 20th Sept 1915	Front Covered by 13th Brigade R.F.A. Two quiet days, with little shelling by the Germans. Work on improving and strengthening existing dug outs in fire & support trenches.	Casualties 19th - 1 killed 20th - 1 Wounded
21st Sept 1915	First day of our Bombardment, which appeared to affect very little reply to this by the Germans. Shrapnel kept up all day at Hohollen parapet, and sniping. Machine guns & Rifles fire all night. Antennae Bombardment	2 Sick reported Batt: Capt Pike app'td G.S.O. 3 4th Corps, Offr'd to take up appointment. Casualties - 1 Killed 2 Sick reported
22nd Sept 1915	Second day of Bombardment.	1 F.A. Casualties - 7 wounded + 1 Pttman 2 killed
23rd Sept 1915	Third day of Bombardment. Artillee Manoeuvering of fire trenches and supports from 6 am to 11 am — Manning the parapet in a few places.	
24th Sept 1915 6.30 p.m.	Fourth day of Bombardment. Commencement of relief of Batts by Bareilly Bde. Batt'ns on relief concentrated as follows:- No 1 Coy RUGBY POST No 2 Coy MIN POST No 3 Coy BRACQUEROT STREET No 4 Coy G.H.Q Trench HQrs in RUE DE BRACQUEROT. Relief completed by 10 pm	Casualties - 1 killed 2 wounded 1 S.O.R. & 2 Wounded myrn L/Col Widdicombe C.O. gone to Indian Corps HQrs to bring Division in touch with. Capt Hawkins assumes command.
25th Sept 1915 5.50	Bareilly & Garhwal Bdes make assault on German line	

Army Form C. 2118.

WAR DIARY
or
INTELLIGENCE SUMMARY.
(Erase heading not required.)

101

Hour, Date, Place	Summary of Events and Information	Remarks and references to Appendices
7.15 am	Batt'n moves forward to concentrate in "B" line as follows:— Nos 2 Coy via River Birdcage Street. HQ, Nos 1 & 4 Coys & HQrs via North Telleby Street. No 3 Coy via South Telleby Street.	Casualties on 25th & 26th September. Killed 7. Wounded 55.
11 am	Batt'n receive orders to move forward and concentrate in firing line & support trenches between North Hooded Gorge Street and North Telleby Street in an attack. Attack orders received from B.G.C. (2059), ordering Batt'n to be in Brigade Reserve between Seaforth Str [?]	3 Subs } Reynolds (Wounded) I.F.A. Capt H L Ainsworth & M Burke wounded
11.30 am	Verbal orders received that attack orders cancelled and Batt'n ordered to take over front line. No 5 "B" in conjunction with 1st Seaforth Hrs. In conformer with this No 1 & 2 Coys took over firing line and supports with 2 platoons No 3 Coy in support on relief from North Telleby St to line S of	
1 pm	No 4 Coy withdrew to Telleby Street and No 3 platoons No 3 to North Compston Trench HQrs in support line at junction with S Telleby St	

Forms/C. 2118/10

WAR DIARY
or
INTELLIGENCE SUMMARY.
(Erase heading not required.)

Army Form C. 2118.

102

Hour, Date, Place	Summary of Events and Information	Remarks and references to Appendices
25th Sept 19.15 4 pm	The Battn. expected move and was prepn.	
6 pm	Orders received to take over line from 2nd Gordons	
7 pm	No 4 Coy moved up to take over immediately, and 2 platoons No 3 Coy forming supports up to South Moated Grange Plant new portion of the line taken up first held by Battn. from MAIN STREET to SOUTH MOATED GRANGE STREET	
9 pm		
26th Sept 19.15 6 am	Hostile Heavy howitzer fire directed at Rugby of line held by Battn. and on the front of attack attempted. This latter was driven in by our Rifle fire	
11 am	No I & B Coys withdrawn to TICKELOY STREET No 2 Coy took over line from No I Coy.	
3 pm	No 2 Coy withdrawn by I Coy 93rd Russn. Inf'y and withdrawn to TICKELOY STREET	
5.30 pm	No 4 Coy withdrawn by I Coy 12th Seaforth Hldrs to TICKELOY STREET. more completed Battn. stood to B Line move completed Battn. in Brigade reserve	

Army Form C. 2118.

WAR DIARY
or
INTELLIGENCE SUMMARY.
(Erase heading not required.)

103

Hour, Date, Place	Summary of Events and Information	Remarks and references to Appendices
27th Sept 1915 7 pm	Battn moved to Endruit Start Point bet GT Windmill CB & reymous Battn ends resumed command	12 sick } Regm Battn 4 wounded
28th Sept 1915		
11 am	Battn relieves 1st Regiment in Fire Trench. H.Q. moves to Crothet Home. Commencement of Relief of Battn by Battn of 60th Brigade (Duchess Light Inf. & Shropshire Light Inf.)	2 Coy 9th Inf attached to Battn. 1 Sick 2 wounded } Regm Battn 2/Lt W MUNRAY 1/4 R & J. PRYER 1/4 R join Battn
7 pm		
29th Sept 1915 1 am	Relief completed	Casualties 1 wounded
3 am	Battn completes move to Rubble in Rugby Road	5 sick 24 wounded } Regm tomwe Dressing stn
8 am	Battn fatigue (carrying cylinders from front line to Rue de Bacquerot)	
4.30 pm	Battn moves to Billets near Rue Chapelle	
30th Sept 1915	Right half Battn was bath at Lestrem	14 sick regm from Bouleraed

G. Williscombe

Lt Col

Comdg 1/4th Gurkha Rifles

121/7601

Serial No. 96.

Confidential

War Diary

of

1/9th Gurkha Rifles.

FROM 1st October 1915 TO 31st October 1915.

Army Form C. 2118.

104

WAR DIARY
or
INTELLIGENCE SUMMARY.
(Erase heading not required.)

Instructions regarding War Diaries and Intelligence Summaries are contained in F. S. Regs., Part II, and the Staff Manual respectively. Title pages will be prepared in manuscript.

Hour, Date, Place.	Summary of Events and Information.	Remarks and references to Appendices
1st October 1915. VIEILLE CHAPELLE	5 pm. C.O. and Adjutant attend conference at Bde Hqrs and receive instructions as to turning into line at FESTUBERT.	
2nd Oct 1915. 10 am	C.O. and Coy Comrs visit H.Q. 10th Worcesters to take over line	
9.45 am	Batts march in the Adjutant to Rivercourt at LE HAMEL via ZELOBES - LOCON BRIDGE.	
5 pm.	Batts move by Companies via RUE DE BOIS - RUE L'EPINETTE to take over IND II.C. in front of FESTUBERT. No 3 A.C. under Lt Duncan attached to 4th Seaforth Hrs Front Orkney Road - to centre of ROTHESAY BAY Firing line has 2 Coy - Capt Paxman Support No 1 Coy - Lt Pryce Reserve No 4 Coy - Capt Hawkins 2 h.G. in line.	21st Trenches taken over by Battn.
9.15 pm.	Relief completed.	
3rd	Trenches wet. The Parapet of Rothesay Bay was weak and very little wise was up in front of our line A quiet day, with a little hostile firing from Willow Farm Nords, both of improving line commenced	Casualties - 2 wounded

Army Form C. 2118.

WAR DIARY
or
INTELLIGENCE SUMMARY.
(Erase heading not required.)

/05

Hour, Date, Place.	Summary of Events and Information.	Remarks and references to Appendices
3rd Oct 1915 H.Qs. No II C.	Rotheray Bay parapet thickened, and the winning of the line undertaken. The improving of others Road, strengthening dug outs and salvaging of timber. Rations brought up by trolley from MARAIS to Reserve line, and from there carried up by Coy in Reserve.	
4th Oct 1915	Nothing of note occurred. 4th Batty RFA covering in front. Work undertaken above continued.	Lieut Hughes } Jan Ralf Yr Field A.A.R. I.G.O. Sub Reg Sury Khwoska +37 D R's Reinforcements arrived to 6 Sikh regn from 1st A. Casualties - 1 wounded
5th Oct 1915 3 pm	Local Relief carried out. No 1 Coy to Firing line No 4 Coy to Support No 2 Coy to Reserve Work continued.	4 Sick } Regn from 8 Wounded } 1st A.
6th Oct 1915 2.30 pm	Reassignment of Bde Front. No 3 Coy relieves by a Coy 4th Seaforth into Reserve with Batt. No 4 Coy taken over Right Half of Rotheray Bay from 4th Seaforth. No 2 Coy moves up into Support.	Casualties 2 wounded 4 Sick 18 Wounded } Regn Jas: Bowditch Marr Jan

Army Form C. 2118.

WAR DIARY
or
INTELLIGENCE SUMMARY.
(Erase heading not required.)

106

Hour, Date, Place.	Summary of Events and Information.	Remarks and references to Appendices
6th Oct 1915. Hqs. IND II.C.	Subsection Ind II.C. now includes front ORKNEY ROAD to STAFFORD Rd.	
7th Oct 1915.	Work of improvements carried out, a quiet day to our front.	
8th Oct 1915. 3 pm	Local Relief No 2 Coy relieved No 1 in Firing Line No 3 " " " to Support No 1 " " " to Reserve by No 2nd G.R. not Line	Casualties – 2 wounded
9th Oct 1915.	No change, work continued. Trench Stores Depots meet in Firing Line. Support and Reserve of 150 grenades and 36 Boxes S.A.A.	
10th Oct 1915.	Work of improvements during better period in H.E.IIC. greatly strengthens the line. The following was our Inspection Trench to ROTHESAY Bay dug. The parapet thickened and improved other Roads improved firing front & Support and Front line trenches cleared up.	1 Sick reported from 1st R.

Army Form C. 2118.

WAR DIARY
or
INTELLIGENCE SUMMARY.
(Erase heading not required.)

107

Hour, Date, Place.	Summary of Events and Information.	Remarks and references to Appendices
HQ 1/4 G.R. 3 p.m. 10th Oct 1915	No 1 Coy took over posts in FESTUBERT from 2nd G.R.	
4.30 p.m.	1 Coy 2nd G.R. moved up to relieve No 4 Coy.	
6.30 p.m.	Remainder of Relief commenced.	
7.30 p.m.	Relief completed and Bn. withdrawn into Estaminet Corner	
HQ. Or Reserve 11th Oct 1915 5 p.m.	Bn. Reserve in Dugouts near Estaminet Corner. Fatigues as under — 100 men under Lt Brunton } To work under G.O. Sappers. 50 men „ „ G.O. 50 „ „ „ „	2 Sick reported from I.G.A.
6 p.m.	1 G.O. + 25 men on carrying fatigue. Work done making roads & trenches to winter use.	
12th Oct 1915 5 p.m. 6 p.m.	2 Fatigues, one of 100 men under Lt Martiney one of 95 men to carry water & Pay in to continue work of previous day.	Casualties — 1 man died of wounds
13th Oct 1915	Bombing Practice by Coys. Hon. Bald. stood to for 2 hours during Smoke Bomb demonstration	1 Sick 1 wounded Reported from 15 A. Casualties 5 wounded 1 killed

Army Form C. 2118.

WAR DIARY
or
INTELLIGENCE SUMMARY.
(Erase heading not required.)

108

Hour, Date, Place.	Summary of Events and Information.	Remarks and references to Appendices
14th Oct 1915. 10 am Estaminet Corner 2 pm 5.45 pm 7.10 pm	C.O. and Coy Comdrs go round had a t with a view to taking over trenches 4th Seaforths then by 1st Coy relieves Coy 1 of 4th Seaforths in front. Batt: have Coy companies to take over from 4th Seaforths. Relief completed Dispositions Right Firing Line No 3 Coy. Lt Hughes Left Firing Line & Support No 2 Coy with 1 Platoon No 4 Coy. Capt Pearson Reserve No 1 Coy, Lt Poynter, No 4 Coy (less 2 Platoons) Capt Hawkinson. GODNEY'S Keep 1 Platoon No 4 Coy 3.1 M Gr 2 M Gs in Firing Line 14th Battery R.F.A covering front. HQrs in old British Line Rations brought up by Lorries to H.Qrs. Work taken in hand. Building up Parapet of Reserve Trench, and dug outs therein. Wiring front of Firing Line & Support and improving parapet of Fire Trench.	22nd Inniskilling [?] Coy Relief Bn [?]

Army Form C. 2118.

WAR DIARY
or
INTELLIGENCE SUMMARY.
(Erase heading not required.)

109

Hour, Date, Place.	Summary of Events and Information.	Remarks and references to Appendices
hs 2.4		
15th Oct 1915	Work taken in hand carried on little wiper on Bluff firm from	4 Pick 4 Wounded men from I.F.A
16th Oct 1915		1 wounded, 1 follower reported from I.F.A.
17th Oct 1915 2 pm	Local Relief carried out No 1 Coy Relieved No 2 Coy No 4 Coy relieved No 3 Coy	
18th Oct 1915	Work carried on to improve line	
19th Oct 1915	Or 10th Warwicks gun and line to arrange relief.	2 Pick 4 wounded men from I.F.A
20th Oct 1915 5.30 pm	Batn relieved by 8th North Staffords, T 10th R Warwicks and moved to Bilaets by Coy on Relief to LA COUTURE. Relief delayed as 10th Royal Warwicks were 2 hours late	
9 pm	Relief Completed	1 Sick reported from I.F.A.
21st Oct 19, 6.10 am	C.O. and Coy Cmdrs Visit trenches CINDER TRACK (finish) 6 HAZARA Trench (end) or RUE DU BOIS in view of relief.	
5.30 pm	Batn moves by Companies to take on another line from 1st J.L.I. and 2/8th Goorkhas	
7.15 pm	Relief Completed. – a very good relief.	

Army Form C. 2118.

WAR DIARY
or
INTELLIGENCE SUMMARY.
(Erase heading not required.)

110

Hour, Date, Place.	Summary of Events and Information.	Remarks and references to Appendices
EDWARD ROAD 21st Oct 19.15	Dispositions. Right: Firing Line & Support No 2 Coy & 2 Platoons No 1 Coy Capt Parsons. Left: Firing Line & Support. No 3 Coy & 1 Platoon No 4 Coy under L. Hughes. Reserve No 1 Coy less 2 Platoons & Support L. Poynton. No 4 Coy less 1 Platoon Capt Hackman No 4 Coy 9. I.M.G. COPSE KEPT 15 men Machine Guns 2 in firing line HQrs. on EDWARD ROAD 94th Batty R.F.A Covering front. Work of sinking sappers in front line, and improving parapet + paradas.	23rd Jan in Trenches. 1st Lieut – LA COUTURE
22nd Oct 19.15	6 + 7th: Relieves relieve 94th Battery on front live and its Trenches by our Ditches Sing Khatri. Reconnaissance of Ditches front by Sub Hakim Sing Khatri. Work on defence Further reconnaissance of Ditches by L. Amgot & others	Casualties – 1 killed 1 Sick reported from 1st R.
23rd Oct 19.15		

Army Form C. 2118.

WAR DIARY
or
INTELLIGENCE SUMMARY.
(Erase heading not required.)

111

Hour, Date, Place.	Summary of Events and Information.	Remarks and references to Appendices
24th Oct 1915 6 pm	Relief of Battn by 69th Punjabis	Casualties. 1 killed 2 Sick rejoined from 1 F.A., 2 wounded
7.30 pm PARADIS (R19)	Relief completed. Battn marches to Billets at PARADIS via FOSSE by Coys	
25th Oct 1915	Rest in Billets. Men clean up equipment etc	L. Poynter gone on 1 weeks leave
26th Oct 1915	Parades commenced daily at 10 am to 3 pm under Company Comdts. Special attention being paid to. (1) Bomb Throwing (2) Physical training, especially doubling (3) Rapid Fire standing with fixed swords hrs 3 - 8 - 9 - 4 - 14 Platoons designated Grenadier Platoons and specially trained under 2 Lieutenant J Grundy officer	2 Sick rejoined from 1 F.A.
27th Oct 1915 4.30 pm	Battn: Parade under Adjutant to practise Ceremonial Drill	L. Kemp gone on 1 weeks leave. Football match v Bttn Signals. Lost 2-1. 2 Sick rejoined from 1 F.A.
	Adjt & Havildars visit sight under Staff Captain for Parade ready for inspection by H.M. The King-Emperor.	
28th Oct 1915 10.30 am	Battn marches to Parade Ground for inspection by H.M. The King-Emperor.	Men lunching over without Rifles.
12 noon	Battn: troops intimated and ordered to return to Billets owing to His Majesties accident previous cancelled.	

Army Form C. 2118.

WAR DIARY
or
INTELLIGENCE SUMMARY.

(Erase heading not required.)

Hour, Date, Place.	Summary of Events and Information.	Remarks and references to Appendices
PARAIS. R.19.		
29th Oct 1915	Parades under Coy Cmdrs	Anniversary of going into Trenches
30th Oct 1915	Right Half Battn. and L.G. detachment used Baths at VIEILLE CHAPELLE. Battn. rests in Billets, Sunday being observed as a Holiday.	Colonel Widdicombe C.B. gone on leave. 2nd Pick rejoin from I.F.A.
31st Oct 1915		Roll call of Battn on 29th showed:- Lt. Widdicombe 3 B. on. Capt. Macpherson Lt. Kemp and 123 other Ranks. left Battn = During the year 29.10.15. Also 32 wounded & rejoined and Lt. Forgan T./05 O.R.1 sick rejoined Total 4 B.Os 280 O.R.1

A.F.Parsons. Capt
Comdg 1/9th Gurkha Rifles.

Serial No. 96.

12/4780

Confidential

War Diary

of

1/9th Gurkha Rifles.

FROM 1st November 1915 TO 30th November 1915

Army Form C. 2118.

WAR DIARY
or
INTELLIGENCE SUMMARY.

(Erase heading not required.)

C.A.
W.D.S.T.
6 DEC 1915 / 3

Hour, Date, Place.	Summary of Events and Information.	Remarks and references to Appendices
PARADIS — R.19 1st Nov 1915. 2nd Nov 1915.	Left Half Battⁿ was the Baths at LESTREM	Capt. Mackenzie 90th & 2nd Lieutenant Brennan Joins
11.45 am	Battⁿ marches to Billets on Road VIEILLE CHAPELLE — LA COUTURE R.34 c.7.9	
	No 4 Coy met 2 Lieut Mowbray moved up to take over posts in rear of Front Line Battⁿs in B⁺ Reserve	1 wounded Rejoins from I.P.A.
R.34 c.7.9 3rd Nov 1915. 4 hr 1915. 10 a.m.	Battⁿ remains in reserve C.O. Adj⁺ & Lieut. Poynder visit line with a view to relieving 1st Seaforths from	2 Lieut. Poynder rejoins from leave 2 Lieut. Mowbray goes on leave 2 Lieut. Fisher goes on leave
2.30 p.m.	No 1 Coy moves by Pelaton to take over Jimmy Line Farm Cover to CINDER TRACK	Casualties 8 Killed 1 Wounded
3 p.m.	No 3 Coy moves to take up support in old British line	
4 p.m.	No 2 Coy moves to take up breastworks in Rue DE BOIS	
5 p.m.	No 4 Coy relieved in posts by 3rd London moves into Reserve in RUE DES BERCEAUX. H.Q.s with Reserve	
6.10 p.m.	Relief completed 14th Battⁿ R.F.A. cover our front. 2nd London Bn by hot Ly duarded into 9 pieces also 6 M. Guns. Trenches very wet have been neglected	

Army Form C. 2118.

WAR DIARY
or
INTELLIGENCE SUMMARY.
(Erase heading not required.)

114

Hour, Date, Place.	Summary of Events and Information.	Remarks and references to Appendices
RUE DE BERCEAUX S.te NOnne 10 am	Officers 4th Seaforth His went line	
3 pm	Relief by 4th Seaforths commences	1 Sick regained from 1.F.A
6.30 pm	Relief completed	
	Batt.s marched by Coys to Billets at CROIX MARMUSE. all Bomb, Sanitary, kindred men to 4th Seaforths	
6th Nov 1915 7 am	R.Q.S for men carrying out	
11 am	Batt.s marched to LESTREM to Entrain	
12 noon	Batt.s entrained 25 men to each Rlwy 29 trips 4 Sick regd from 1FA	
3.10 pm	Batt.s detrained at MORBECQUE and marched	
	to Billets at LE Gd HASARD	
LE Gd HASARD.	Batt.s rests in Billets and cleans up clothing +	
7th Nov 1915	equipment	
8th Nov 1915	Parades under Coy Comdrs	
9th Nov 1915	Parades under Coy Comdrs S. Mothers, Musketry, trials	1 Sick regd from IFA. Capt. Mackenzie reptd
10th Nov 1915	Parades under Coy Comdrs	St Divisional Sigs from (Capt Paunam & ?hypnor att to
11th Nov 1915	Parades as above. Gen Jacouet Comp. Reviewed Div. Drew with	
12th Nov 1915	Officers Company Parades	1 Sick regd from IFA
13th Nov 1915	Batt.s marches in mass of 1st Seaforth Hgs in rear	Capt Paunam & ?hyp rejnd from leave
9.45 am	to LIERES via MORBECQUE - ST VENANT - BUSNES -	
	LILLERS. 6 new Billets - about 16 miles arrive 1.20 pm	

Army Form C. 2118.

Instructions regarding War Diaries and Intelligence Summaries are contained in F. S. Regs., Part II, and the Staff Manual respectively. Title pages will be prepared in manuscript.

WAR DIARY
or
INTELLIGENCE SUMMARY.
(Erase heading not required.)

115

Hour, Date, Place.	Summary of Events and Information.	Remarks and references to Appendices
LIERES – 14th Nov 1915 / 15th Nov 1915	Battn rests in Billets. Parades at 10 am under Coy Comdrs. Skirmishing & extending order drill.	Football match Battn v Signal Battn Left S. Bgd.
16th Nov 1915.	Parades as on 15th.	Football match officers 1st Battn v officers 1st Seaforth Hdrs. Lost 3-2
17th Nov 1915.	Parades as on 16th. Continued with Coy Route marches	2/ Forsyth returns 2 4 days leave
4 p.m.	Genl Jacob visits Battn & gives the officers to say goodbye before leaving the Division	Lieut Berry goes on 4 days leave
18th Nov 1915. 9.45 a.m.	Battn moves Billets to FONTAINES LES HERMANS & LES HERMANS.	
LES HERMANS 20th Nov 1915 / 21st Nov 1915 / 22nd Nov 1915 / 23rd Nov 1915	NIDONCHELLE via AMES. Company Parades. Coy Parades. All officers needed from leave – Coy Parades.	Capt Parrump goes on leave & Suite resigns from I.S.R.
11.45 a.m.	Battn marches to LILLERS & entrains for MARSEILLES.	
6.30 p.m.	From left LILLERS. Corps Comdr Genl Sir C. Anderson & Battn. While entraining and said Goodbye to officers British and Gurkha	Capt Paurrow & Lt Berry rejoining Battn from leave at Abbeville.
24th Nov 1915 / 25th Nov 1915	Battn in train en route to MARSEILLES. Route via ST POL – ABBEVILLE – AMIENS – VILLENEUVE ST GEORGES NEVERS – LE TIEL – PONT AVIGNON	

Army Form C. 2118.

116

WAR DIARY
or
INTELLIGENCE SUMMARY.
(Erase heading not required.)

Instructions regarding War Diaries and Intelligence Summaries are contained in F. S. Regs., Part II, and the Staff Manual respectively. Title pages will be prepared in manuscript.

Hour, Date, Place.	Summary of Events and Information.	Remarks and references to Appendices
26ᵗʰ Nov 1915. 1 a.m.	Battⁿ arrived at MARSEILLES at ARENC Station and detrained, marching to Camp SANTI. 1ˢᵗ line Quarter made arranged for collection of Bau kits to ABBATTOIR Camp.	
19 a.m	at MARSEILLES with D.A.R.G.	
3 p.m	C.O. and adjutant visit Camp MUSSOTT. to select new position to bring up strength of Battⁿ. Reinforcements to bring up (strength of Battⁿ) to 808. (10 p.c. over F.S. Strength)	(14 of own men returned to Mayonne & Rgtl Puniter. Coy & mule.)
27ᵗʰ Nov 1915.	Capt Blandt and 43 Reinforcements join Battⁿ.	
28ᵗʰ Nov 1915.	Battⁿ prepares for entrainment.	
29ᵗʰ Nov 1915.	20 unfit men sent to MUSSOTT.	
	13 O.R. join from MUSSOTT	
10 a.m.	Coy Route march	
30ᵗʰ Nov 1915.	Battⁿ inspected by Brigadier.	
11 a.m	1ˢᵗ line Transport ready to entrain.	

Allanhurriwata
Commanding 1/9 G.R.
Captain
Commanding 1/9 G.R.